Demons *yes - but thank God for good* Angels

By LEHMAN STRAUSS

The First Person
The Second Person
The Third Person

The Prophecies of Daniel
Devotional Studies in Galatians
and Ephesians
James Your Brother
The Epistles of John
The Book of the Revelation

Certainties for Today
The Eleven Commandments
We Live Forever

Demons, Yes—but Thank God
for Good Angels

Lehman Strauss

Demons yes— but thank God for good Angels

LOIZEAUX BROTHERS
Neptune, New Jersey

FIRST EDITION, FEBRUARY 1976
SECOND PRINTING, JUNE 1976

Library of Congress Cataloging in Publication Data

Strauss, Lehman.
    Demons, yes—but thank God for good angels.

    1. Devil. 2. Angels. I. Title.
BT981.S77   235   75-38804
ISBN 0-87213-831-3

        Printed in the United States of America

CONTENTS

THE GOD OF THIS WORLD

Millions living on the earth today are witnessing an amazing interest in psychic phenomena. Millions more are involved in it. Obviously there is a spiritual vacuum in the lives of many which cries out for fulfillment. Never has there been such an expressed desire on the part of so many to want to know the future. Our deteriorating society has created a growing fear of what might come to pass. Even those politicians and statesmen who are predicting better times ahead know they are whistling in the dark.

MAN'S SEARCH FOR AN ANSWER

There is an emptiness in the hearts of millions that craves satisfaction. We know that this emptiness is the result of a widespread departure from the Christian faith. An extra-Biblical liberal theology has invaded many denominational colleges and seminaries, and this in turn has placed in many pulpits men who have no answer for the hungry hearts of those who attend the church of their choice. Because the present-day church has apostatized from the faith, multitudes are seeking help from other sources.

There are two supernatural forces contending for the mastery of man; they are God and Satan. Both cannot control a person at the same time. So when a man abandons God, the force of evil will take control. One of the characteristics of the "latter times," and an astounding aspect of Biblical prophecy, is the increase of demon activity. In a most solemn and specific prediction, the divinely-inspired penman wrote, "Now the spirit speaketh expressly, that in the latter times some shall depart from the faith, giving heed to seducing spirits, and doctrines of devils [demons]" (1 Timothy 4:1).

The time period of increased demon activity is upon us. More and more these wicked agencies are getting a stranglehold upon the lives of young people and older alike. Departure from the true Christian faith, as it is revealed in the Word of God, is making it increasingly easy for demonic spirits to take over. Witches and clairvoyants are becoming as common as psychiatrists and psychologists. Every phase of human society is being invaded by evil spirits.

Recently I browsed in a bookstore in a small Pennsylvania town with a population of 7,000. I counted fifty-nine titles dealing with various phases of the occult: the crystal ball, astrology, tarot-card reading, witchcraft, spiritism, prophecy, the ouija board, and horoscopes.

The general idea behind the word "occult" suggests hidden knowledge. When a man forsakes the knowledge of God, he has but one other source of knowledge, the occult. He cannot have peace of mind so long as his future is uncertain, so he pursues that knowledge that has evaded him. But whether or not he is aware of it, all occult activity is Satan-controlled.

HOW IT ALL BEGAN

There is one major destructive lie which is the basis of the whole satanic system. Our Lord Jesus Christ stated it clearly in His scathing accusation against some religious leaders of His day. Note His solemn words: "Ye are of your father the devil, and the lusts of your father ye will do. He was a murderer from the beginning, and abode not in the truth, because there is no truth in him. When he speaketh a [the] lie, he speaketh of his own [i.e., of himself]: for he is a liar, and the father of it" (John 8:44).

The Authorized Version has failed to include the definite article in connection with the word "lie." It should read *"the* lie," as the Greek text states. There is one specific lie, and the devil is the father of *"it."* Simply stated, *"the* lie" is the denial of God and the deifying of the creature (or the created being).

The first created being to apostatize from God was the angel Lucifer when he said, "I will be like the most High" (Isaiah 14:14). It was this rebellion of Lucifer whereby he became the devil. The lie is that the creature no longer needs God, and therefore he becomes his own god. He deliberately cuts himself off from the knowledge of God, which is the only true knowledge, containing the only accurate information about the future. An article in *Time* (June 19, 1972) said, "Much of the occult, after all, is man's feeble attempt to become godlike, to master the world around him."

Many conservative Bible scholars believe that the origin of demons is associated with the fall of Lucifer when he became Satan. The Lord Jesus spoke of "the devil and his angels" (Matthew 25:41), suggesting that possibly they followed him when he conceived and perpetrated "the lie." The Apostle John spoke of "the dragon . . . and his angels" (Revelation 12:7). These rebellious fallen angels are the demons who accepted the lie. They are intelligent beings who are under the leadership of Satan, their commander-in-chief. They possess superhuman intelligence and superphysical strength. These are the wicked spirits, the rulers of the darkness of this world who are contending for mastery over the bodies and minds of all members of the human race.

Having succeeded in taking a host of angels captive by means of "the lie," the devil proceeded to invade the human race. Man is God's highest creation, having been created in the image and likeness of God (Genesis 1:26-27), so man was Satan's next prize to conquer. He came to Eve when she was alone. Both Adam and Eve had been warned by God that they should not eat of the tree of the knowledge of good and evil, the penalty for disobedience being death (Genesis 2:17). But Satan said, "[But] God doth know that in the day ye eat thereof, then your eyes shall be opened, and ye shall be as gods [Elohim], knowing good and evil" (Genesis 3:5).

In substance the devil said, "Abandon God and all that He says, then you will be like God. You will become your own god, 'knowing . . . .' " Then and there "the lie" invaded the human race, and Satan captured his next prize. Adam agreed to go along with Eve in her decision to yield to Satan, and their fall resulted in the fall of their posterity (Romans 5:12, 17,19).

Today unregenerate mankind is without the knowledge of God. His world is crumbling about him. His fears and anxieties are driving him to a state of frustration. In his search for the hidden knowledge that eludes him, he turns to the occult which is Satan's world. But the devil's world is the kingdom of darkness (Revelation 16:10). His demons are called "the rulers of the darkness of this world" (Ephesians 6:12). Anyone who becomes involved in the evil practice of sorcery will immediately become victim of the "unfruitful works of darkness" (Ephesians 5:11).

No passage in the Bible expresses this fact more clearly than Romans, chapter one. Before ever God gave to man the written revelation in the Scriptures, man had a witness within himself, his *conscience* (1:19; 2:15), plus the witness of God around him, *creation* (1:20). Though man's knowledge of God was limited, nevertheless he "knew God" (1:21). But men suppressed the truth (1:18) and "did not like to retain God in their knowledge" (1:28).

Now take a close look at verse 25: "who changed *the truth* of God into a [the] *lie*, and worshipped and served the creature more [rather] than the Creator .... " The two contrasting forces here are "the truth" and "the lie." Jesus Christ is "the truth" (John 14:6), and Satan is "the lie" (John 8:44). When any person turns his back on "the truth" he will follow "the lie." The "creature" men are worshiping and serving is the devil. Our society is reaping the bitter consequences, having sunk to a new low in immorality, lawlessness, murder, rape, and all sorts of evil practices. Beginning with homosexuality the Romans passage lists the wicked deeds in a society where people turn from Christ to Satan, from "the truth" to "the lie" (1:26-32). There can be no denial of the fact that the growing interest in Satanism, in its many forms, is corrupting our society more and more. Involvement in the occult is the major cause of the growing disorder in our world. Occultly subjected people do strange and wicked things.

SATAN—THE GOD OF THIS WORLD

The meaning of the weird happenings in today's world can be explained only by understanding the powers behind them. The Apostle Paul affirmed that our basic conflict is not with "flesh and blood, but against principalities, against powers, against the rulers of the darkness of this world, against spiritual wickedness [i.e., wicked spirits] in high places" (Ephesians 6:12). The Bible indicates that the atmospheric and stellar heavens surrounding planet earth are filled with hostile spirit beings. These spirits are invisible, but intelligent and influential. Their chief is "Beelzebub the prince of the devils" (Matthew 12:24). (Beelzebub is one of the several names given to Satan.) It cannot be denied that in the sixties and seventies we have been witnessing an upsurge of demon activity. The lawlessness and licentiousness of these present times is unprecedented in modern civilization. It seems that these wicked forces are mobilizing for an all-out attack.

I am convinced that the growing international conspiracy, which opposes all that is decent and honorable, is satanic. This evil aggression is aimed at every phase of our human civilization. The Scriptures teach plainly that "the whole world lieth in wickedness" (or, the wicked one) (1 John 5:19). A popular religious song would have us believe that God has the whole world in His hands, but that is Satan's lie, and many Christians believe it. Now we know that God is sovereign; however the Bible tells in unmistakable language that the devil has the unregenerated masses in his hands. Jesus stated this repeatedly when He referred to the devil as "the prince of this world" (John 12:31; 14:30; 16:11). Paul wrote,"The god of this world hath blinded the minds of them which believe not" (2 Corinthians 4:4).

In the five verses just mentioned (John 12:31; 14:30; 16:11; 2 Corinthians 4:4; 1 John 5:19), the word "world" is mentioned in each. It will be worth taking the time for a look at the New Testament Greek words translated "world."

The first word is *kosmos.* It is used in at least three different ways. In a number of passages it means the round planet earth on which man has his existence. In such passages the Revised Version sometimes substitutes the word "earth." (See Matthew 5:14; 13:38; Acts 17:24; etc.) When John wrote of Jesus that "He was in the *world*" (John 1:10), he was referring to this planet earth. It is this world, the earth, which is the scene of the prophesied demonic activity.

The *second* usage of the word *kosmos* refers to the

inhabitants of this world, or earth. Both of these first two usages appear together in one verse: "He was in the *world* [earth], and the *world* [earth] was made by Him, and the *world* [the inhabitants of the earth] knew Him not" (John 1:10). This world of mankind is the world God loves. Jesus said, "For God so loved the world" (John 3:16). However, there is that segment of the world of mankind that is alienated from God (Ephesians 2:12; 4:18) and hostile to Christ and His followers. Our Lord said, "If the *world* hate you, ye know that it hated Me before it hated you" (John 15:18). So then it is this unregenerated world of mankind through whom the demons will accomplish their wicked deeds.

The *third* use of the word *kosmos* in Scripture refers to the combined activities, affairs, advantages, and accumulated assets of worldly men on the earth. The Bible calls all these "the things that are in the world" (1 John 2:15), "this world's good" (1 John 3:17). This usage of *kosmos* is not limited to material things, but it includes abstract things which have spiritual and moral (or immoral) values. Paul warns the believer to beware of "the wisdom of this world" (1 Corinthians 1:20; 2:6; 3:19), "the spirit of the world" (2:12), and "the fashion of this world" (7:31). Peter wrote of "the corruption that is in the world" (2 Peter 1:4), and "the pollutions of the world" (2:20).

Dr. Merrill Unger made note of the fact that "In more than thirty important passages the Greek word 'kosmos' . . . is employed in the New Testament to portray the whole mass, of unregenerate men alienated from God, hostile to Christ, and organized governmentally as a system or federation under Satan (John 7:7; 14:27; 1 Corinthians 1:21; 11:32; 1 Peter 5:9; 1 John 3:1,13; *et al.*"

The second Greek word is *aion.* It likewise is translated *world.* However, it connotes the idea of time and is more accurately rendered "age." The disciples questioned Jesus about "the end of the *world* [age]" (Matthew 24:3), speaking of that time when He would return to the earth. Paul used the same word when he wrote of our Lord Jesus Christ, "Who gave Himself for our sins, that He might deliver us from this present evil *world* [age]" (Galatians 1:4). This present *aion,* from Pentecost to the return of Christ, is described as "evil."

CHRISTIAN, BEWARE!

There is, then, an organized and orderly system of evil, designated in the Bible as "the world." Behind this system there is an intelligent, supernatural mind which rules. This ruler is Satan who, with the aid of his demons, controls men in this present age. Christians who have not had this Biblical teaching are too often deceived in these matters. Many who claim faith in Jesus Christ have no understanding of the world that surrounds them and the unseen powers behind that world order. We live in the midst of an evil system that is controlled by God's enemies. So let us heed those solemn exhortations which warn us to "Love not the *world,* neither the things that are in the *world.* If any man love the *world,* the love of the Father is not in him" (1 John 2:15). The Christian is "to keep himself unspotted from the *world"* (James 1:27), because "the friendship [with] the *world* is enmity with God" (James 4:4).

Now I cannot think of any area of life more subtle in its appeal than the occult. While speaking in California I learned of a husband and wife who were faced with a serious problem. They were struggling with an important decision which involved a move from the United States to a country in Asia. The husband was a trained scientist who had been offered a lucrative position. He was eager to accept the new position and venture the move, but his wife had strong doubts and even fear about leaving the United States. She had spent many sleepless nights, and in addition she was unable to hold her food. This couple went to a pastor for help. After two counseling sessions the pastor concluded that the young wife's problem was fear of the future. She felt she needed some assuring word that, if she went to Asia, all would be well. The pastor, a man with theological training, unwisely suggested to the couple that they see an astrologer, who made the claim of possessing insight to the future. The pastor should have known better, because he was sending that young woman into Satan's territory. She wanted to discover hidden knowledge about her future, the problem many people face today. Fortunately we had the Word of God with which to minister to that young woman's need. She was rescued from the power of darkness.

The Christian is forbidden to go to Satan's world for anything. What did Satan say to Eve in the garden of Eden? "Abandon God from your thinking, then you will be like God, *knowing* . . . ." (Genesis 3:5)

Yes, one can get knowledge by subjecting oneself to the devil, but all knowledge gained by means of occult phenomena, whether it be astrology, fortunetelling, spiritism, or magic, is knowledge gained in an ungodly way. No good can ever result from this. Christian, beware! The practice of occultism in any form is a sin.

"If any of you lack wisdom, let him ask of God, that giveth to all men liberally, and upbraideth not; and it shall be given him" (James 1:5).

"Regard not them that have familiar spirits, neither seek after wizards, to be defiled by them: I am the LORD your God" (Leviticus 19:31).

Beware of the peril of occult deception. There is a forecast of the future in the Holy Scripture. But if you abandon God's truth and expose yourself to the false prognosticators of the future, you will be left with an empty form of religion lacking God's power. All occultists are evil. "From such turn away" (2 Timothy 3:5). Give the Word of God first place in your life. The Bible rightly understood and obeyed is the Christian's only protection against any and all satanic deception.

SATAN'S INFLUENCE IN GOVERNMENTS

It seems incredible that Satan and his demons should be given liberty to roam as freely as they do. And yet, many and varied are their activities. We have seen how Satan's main sphere of operation is in the realm of religion. However, we cannot fail to see how influential these evil spirits are in world governments. The Scriptures teach clearly and unmistakably that heads of nations are influenced by Satan in the decisions they make. He is most active in this role. With ultimate defeat staring them in the face, the forces of evil are mobilized so as to direct world affairs.

Man in his state of rebellion against God is in league with evil spirits. He might not be aware of it, and he will no doubt deny it, yet it is true. Normal men would not have dared to do what many national rulers have done if they were not controlled by evil spirits. The problems in governments, whether within a single nation or between nations, are but an outward manifestation of a titanic conflict being carried on in the spirit world. Unscrupulous dictators and blood-thirsty warmongers are all under the control of "the prince of this world" (John 12:31; 14:30: 16:11), "the god of this world" (2 Corinthians 4:4), "the prince of the power of the air" (Ephesians 2:2).

We humans can see only "flesh and blood," so we cry out against human wickedness. But to all who are taught by divine revelation, there is given the knowledge that the conflict is "against principalities, against powers, against the rulers of the darkness of this world, against spiritual wickedness [wicked spirits] in high places" (Ephesians 6:12). The unsaved are under the control of satanic and demonic leadership, an organized system of evil which exercises authority over the governments of earth. World rulers provide an ideal base for Satan's operations. "The whole world [the satanic system] lieth in [the wicked one]" (1 John 5:9). Wherever men are, there is "where Satan's seat [throne] is" (Revelation 2:13). The spirit of Satan, which dominates the whole world system, keeps the nations in continuous upheaval.

ANCIENT EGYPT WAS DEMON CONTROLLED

The Pharaoh of Egypt was an idolater under the control of evil spirits. In the time of Moses, at least, almost everything was associated with "gods" (evil spirits). The judgment of the plagues was actually God's judgment upon the "gods" (evil spirits) that controlled the people. God had said, "Against all the gods of Egypt I will execute judgment: I am the LORD" (Exodus 12:12). The word "gods" here is more accurately rendered "princes." The "prince" here is not a human being but an evil spirit who would control a principality.

A normal man would not behave as did Pharaoh. Throughout the entire story in Exodus there are repeated references to Pharaoh's league with magicians and sorcerers of Egypt. A normal unsaved man would not defy God openly: "Who is the LORD, that I should obey His voice?" (Exodus 5:2) This blasphemous challenge can be explained only by the fact that the "gods" (or princes) of Egypt controlled the man. The contest in Egypt was not one between Jehovah and puny man, but between the one true God and the false gods (evil spirits) who controlled the leaders of that nation.

Each time God struck Egypt with a plague it was a blow against the evil forces that held Pharaoh in their control. Had Pharaoh turned to God and repented, the plagues would have ceased. But Pharaoh turned to the evil spirits for help (Exodus 7:11). "It is interesting to study the characters of these pagan 'priests' (Exodus 7:11). In the Hebrew, 'wise men' are called *chakam,* sly or cunning (something akin to sleight-of-hand). The Hebrew for 'sorcerers' is *kashaph,* a 'whisperer' of magic spells. For 'magicians' the Hebrew is *chartom,* literally a horoscopist. Are these three not the identical stock-in-trade of modern religions and superstitions? Surely Satan and his hosts have not changed their methods, but have merely adapted themselves to a changing environment. The trickery is still the same. And Pharaoh was apparently willing to be impressed.

"The Authorized Version gives a wrong impression as to how Pharaoh's heart was hardened. In Exodus 7:13 and subsequent passages, the rendering should be 'Pharaoh's heart was hardened,' without any reference to Jehovah. It definitely suggests the work of evil spirits who kept on deceiving the misguided monarch and causing him to act so strangely contrary to revealed truth" (C. Theodore Schwarze, *The Program of Satan,* pp. 151-152).

ANCIENT PERSIA WAS DEMON CONTROLLED

When historians write their books they fail to take into account the fact that spirit forces play a prominent part in the affairs of men. Non-Christian writers are silent on the interaction between demons and human personalities. Had these writers studied and believed the Bible they would have known about Satan's program and his power to exercise authority over governmental leaders.

They were not mere empty words that Satan spoke when he said to our Lord, "All these things [the kingdoms of the world, and the glory of them] will I give Thee, if Thou wilt fall down and worship me" (Matthew 4:8-9). Luke adds Satan's words, "For that is delivered unto me; and to whomsoever I will I give it" (Luke 4:6). He acquired dominion of the earth from our first parents when he caused their fall in the garden of Eden. Satan has continued his control over unregenerate mankind, and some of his greatest achievements are through the heads of world governments.

A few verses of Scripture in the book of Daniel give us a rare glimpse into the unseen world of spirit forces. "Then said he unto me, Fear not, Daniel: for from the first day that thou didst set thine heart to understand, and to chasten thyself before thy God, thy words were heard, and I am come for thy words. But the prince of the kingdom of Persia withstood me one and twenty days: but, lo, Michael, one of the chief princes, came to help me; and I remained there with the kings of Persia . . . . Then said he, Knowest thou wherefore I come unto thee? and now will I return to fight with the prince of Persia: and when I am gone forth, lo, the prince of Grecia shall come" (Daniel 10:12-13,20).

The subject in the context is the unseen struggle between the holy angels and the fallen angels. Here is revealed a conflict about which most people in our civilized world know little.

Daniel had been praying to God about the distressed state of his people the Jews. In answer to his prayer, God dispatched one of His holy angels to come to minister to the aging Daniel. But strangely, while Daniel was praying and fasting, a conflict was underway in the unseen spirit world. An evil angel opposed the coming of God's holy angel, and for twenty-one days he struggled to prevent the holy angel from reaching Daniel. The evil angel is called "the prince of the kingdom of Persia" (Daniel 10:13).

We may dismiss at once the idea that the "prince" is Cyrus, the king of Persia, or some other prince of Persian lineage. As a matter of fact, he is not a man at all. No mere man would be a match for an angel. If one angel was able to slay 185,000 men in the Assyrian army, surely no one man, no matter how great his strength, could withstand one of God's holy ones (2 Kings 19:35; Isaiah 37:36). Neither Cyrus the man, the king of Persia, nor any other man, was somewhere in outer space struggling with one of God's angels enroute from Heaven to earth.

The prince here is an *angel*-prince, one of the evil angels called demons in the New Testament. The term "principalities" appears no less than eight times (Romans 8:38; Ephesians 1:21; 3:10; 6:12; Colossians 1:16; 2:10,15; Titus 3:1). The Greek word *arche* means government or rule, and is used of supramundane beings who control and govern. In some smaller countries the ruler is called the prince, and the area over which he rules is called his principality. Jesus called Satan "the prince of this world" (John 12:31; 14:30; 16:11), and twice Satan is called "the prince of devils" [or demons] (Matthew 9:34; 12:24). Satan has assigned a demon-prince over every principality. Those evil beings are called "the rulers of the darkness of this world" (Ephesians 6:12). These evil spirits animate nations by controlling the minds and actions of men who rule in those nations.

Dr. H. C. Leupold says of these evil powers, "They struggle behind the struggles that are written on the pages of history. They explain the satanic evil that often comes to light under the things that appear on the surface. Since a particular 'prince of the kingdom of Persia' is mentioned (Daniel 10:13), it seems to be a valid conclusion that every heathen nation is dominated by some such prince. Whether each evil angel may have but one nation as his domain, or whether there may be broader spheres of activity in which the more powerful among them are active, we shall hardly be able to decide on the basis of scriptural evidence . . . . The sum of the matter is this: There are powerful forces of evil at work in and through the nations and their rulers to defeat and to overthrow the people of God. This may alarm and cause terror when one considers how powerful these demon potentates are. On the other hand, there are still more powerful agents of good at work, who, by harmonious cooperation, will prevail over their wicked opponents. So the cause of the kingdom is in good hands, and its success is assured" (*Exposition of Daniel*, pp. 458-460).

Supplementary to what is said in Daniel 10:12-13, further attention is given to the conflict between the good and bad angels. Verse 20 continues, "And now will I return to fight the . . . prince of Persia: and when I am gone forth, lo, the prince of Grecia shall come" (Daniel 10:20). The good angel will now return to the place in the heavens to retain the position he won over the *demon*-prince of Persia. But he warns Daniel that when the conflict ceases with Persia, then "the prince of Grecia shall come." Demonic influences were to control the leaders of Greece in the all-out effort to destroy Israel.

DEMONISM IN ANCIENT BABYLON

Daniel, chapter 3, records an incident in ancient Babylon suggesting the presence of evil forces. It is a straightforward account of a pagan king who was inspired to force all of the subjects in his kingdom to do reverence to false gods (evil spirits). Nebuchadnezzar erected a huge image, a figure of a human being. Attended by carefully planned pomp and pageantry, a gala ceremony of worship was planned. When the band began to play, everybody was expected to fall down and worship the image. Only Satan could have been behind such a scheme. Jehovah had forbidden the making and worshiping of other gods (Exodus 20:1-5). Satan turns man from the one true God to worship creatures and created things (Genesis 3:5; Matthew 4:8-9; Romans 1:25; 2 Corinthians 4:4). The demon-prince of Babylon had so completely controlled that nation's monarch as to lead the entire nation into Satan-worship. The whole plan had both religious and political significance. It is a clear-cut case of a great world power under Satan's control.

DEMONS AND GOVERNMENTS TODAY

The curtain is drawn aside and light is now thrown upon strange and startling happenings in international affairs. The upheaval within countries and between nations cannot be reasonably explained from the human standpoint. The disturbances witnessed by people living today cannot be accounted for apart from the mighty invisible forces. These forces are demonic.

In 1929 Clarence Larkin wrote, "If Satan has a 'Prince of Persia' and a 'Prince of Grecia,' why not a prince for every nation? Satan has his limitations. He is not omnipresent, neither is he omnipotent or omniscient. He has to depend upon his agents. And so great and powerful are his 'princes' that it takes a supernatural being, like Michael the archangel, to overcome them."

Ephesians 6:12 is a most significant passage in our present study. Following is the verse taken from the New International Version. Paul wrote, "For our struggle is not against flesh and blood, but against the rulers, against the authorities, against the powers of this dark world and against the spiritual forces of evil in the heavenly realms."

It is clear from this verse that Satan has a strong hold on the kingdom of planet earth. The struggle against evil spirits is a desperate one. In their method of combat they are "authorities" with superhuman power. We are not confronted with mere men or world rulers, but with men who are controlled by these ruling wicked powers, forces of depravity, lawlessness, and moral evil. The leader of these forces is Satan, and men are in subjection to him and his demons. These evil spirits reign over nations on earth.

Ephesians 6:12 contains weighty words divinely inspired. It seems to me that there are many Christians today who live defeated lives because they are either ignorant of what this passage teaches or else they have never read it. The child of God who takes the Christian life seriously knows there are strange powers militating against the Lord Jesus Christ and His followers. The deteriorating and demoralizing trends in world governments are not to be wondered at; God has spelled it out clearly in His Word. The spirit world is unseen with our physical eyes, but the evil effects are visible on every hand. We had better take Paul's words seriously. This whole earth is a battleground. A myriad of demonic hordes are on the march.

There are human rulers who hold high political office and are the unwitting tools of demons. Every politician who has a self-centered philosophy of life, who aspires to possessions, popularity, power, and prestige, is a puppet controlled by evil spirits. By energizing and regulating world leaders, the evil spirits are able to influence world events. High-ranking government officials have been found guilty of involvement in sex scandals, pay-offs, graft, lying, and cheating. Our own nation has been plagued with such events as Chappaquidick, Watergate, and the forced resignation of a vice president and president. I believe that these conditions can be traced to the fact that highly educated men of wealth and influence are influenced in their behavior and decisions by the powers of evil.

In 1952 Dr. Merrill F. Unger published some comments issued by an underground movement of German youth under Hitler's regime: "Every word out of Hitler's mouth is a lie. If he says peace, he means war, and if he calls frivolously on the name of the Almighty, he means the power of evil, the fallen angel, the devil. His mouth is the stinking throat of hell, and his power is fundamentally rotten. Certainly one has to fight against the Nazi terror state with rational weapons, but whoever still doubts the real existence of demonical powers has not understood the metaphysical background of this war. Behind the concrete and perceptible things behind all real and logical considerations, there is the irrational, there is the fight against the demon, against the messenger of Anti-Christ. Everywhere and at all times the demons have lurked in the dark for the hour when man becomes weak, when he arbitrarily abandons his human situation in the world order founded by God for him on freedom .... After the first voluntary downward step he is compelled to the second and third with rapidly increasing speed; but everywhere, and at all times of the greatest human distress, men and women who have retained their freedom have risen as prophets and saints, and called on men to turn back to God. Certainly man is free, but he is unprotected against evil without the living God; he is like a boat without oars, exposed to the tempest, or like a baby without a mother, or like a cloud which dissolves" (Dr. Merrill F. Unger, *Biblical Demonology,* pp. 197-198).

The student of history who has read carefully the life of Adolf Hitler must conclude that the man was driven by strange powers of evil. His ideas about the weakness and wickedness of the Jewish race and the supremacy of the German race would have to be satanically oriented. A cursory reading of the Old Testament reveals the fact that the Jew was a race specially chosen by God, and that every attempt to annihilate the Jews was plotted by pagan rulers who refused to acknowledge Jehovah. I personally read every word of Hitler's *Mein Kampf,* and I am convinced the man was demon possessed.

In 1929, with the arrival of the great economic crisis, the Hitler movement became the strongest dynamic force in the history of Germany. In 1934 Hitler ordered the death of all radical leaders in his own SS. He actually murdered in cold blood every man he suspected did not agree wholeheartedly with all of his ideas. Such action is taken only by a person under Satan's control (John 8:44; 1 John 3:12). The *demon*-prince of Germany was at work.

The period of greatest catastrophe for the Jews commenced in 1933, with Hitler's rise to power. At his command more than six million Jews were put to death by the Nazis, an estimated nine billion dollars worth of Jewish property was plundered. Close to one million Jewish industrial and commercial enterprises were plundered or destroyed. In paroxysms of anger this demon-possessed man did what no ordinary human being would ever think of doing. Studies in philosophy and sociology will not help us understand why some persons behave as they do. The one Book that gives to man the true cause of such behavior is God's Word.

The Biblical doctrine of demons, and the methods by which they operate, provide the only accurate information as to the causes of upheavals in the world. Moreover, there is no solution to the world's problems without that basic knowledge of satanic forces revealed in the Bible, God's Word. We are not surprised when non-Christian heads of state come to invalid conclusions through the exercise of poor judgment. The entire political environment, apart from God and His Word, is full of demonism. We have no justification for looking for solutions to the problems on planet earth before the coming great exorcism. As long as Satan and his evil spirits are at liberty to control the bodies and minds of men and women, world conditions will become increasingly worse.

But there is hope for all and any person in public office. There are some God-fearing people in top spots in government. They are not controlled by evil spirits but by the Holy Spirit. Our world needs more like them. There is only one way for the children of the devil to become God's children. Every unsaved person must personally and experientially receive Jesus Christ as Saviour and Lord (John 1:12; Acts 16:31). The moment the sinner comes to Christ in this way, he is delivered "from the power of darkness, and . . . translated into the kingdom of His [God's] dear Son" (Colossians 1:13).

Any world leader can be set free from Satan and brought to Jesus Christ. "The Lord is . . . not willing that any should perish, but that all should come to repentance" (2 Peter 3:9). Therefore we Christians should obey the exhortation which says, "I exhort therefore, that, first of all, supplications, prayers, intercessions, and giving of thanks, be made for all men; For kings, and for all that are in authority; that we may lead a quiet and peaceable life in all godliness and honesty. For this is good and acceptable in the sight of God our Saviour; Who will have all men to be saved, and to come unto the knowledge of the truth" (1 Timothy 2:1-4).

KILLERS AND LIARS

Anyone who writes about the subject which I have undertaken in this chapter must have a strange feeling in his mind. I am well aware of the fact that there are those who will think me mistaken and misguided. I can understand sympathetically why they might feel as they do. However, no one can argue the point that our planet earth is not the same world in which God placed Adam and Eve. Something has gone wrong.

MURDER IS SATANIC

While waiting in an airport for my plane to arrive, I browsed in the airport bookstore. On the front page of a tabloid paper there appeared in bold print this statement: "Oswald Was Possessed by the Devil When He Shot JFK" (*Midnight,* April 1, 1974). The above statement is correct. The Lord Jesus Christ declared it nineteen hundred years ago when He said, "He [the devil] was a murderer from the beginning" (John 8:44).

The "murderer" (Greek, *anthropoktonos*) means a slayer or killer of men. From the beginning of his history as the devil, he had murder in his heart. Jesus had just said to His accusers, "Ye seek to kill Me" (John 8:40), then He added, "Ye are of your father the devil" (verse 44). Anyone reading this passage will not miss the point Jesus made, namely murderers have kinship with Satan. The devil is characteristically a murderer and the real father of all murderers. The person with a lust to kill is the slave of Satan.

THE FIRST HUMAN MURDERER

Satan was the instigator of the first recorded murder. We read in the Genesis account that "Cain rose up against . . . his brother, and slew him" (Genesis 4:8). The New Testament states clearly that "Cain was of that wicked one, and slew his brother" (1 John 3:12). The "wicked one" is Satan.

The word "slew" (Greek, *sphazo*) is a specialized word which means to butcher or slaughter by cutting the throat. The first murderer learned to kill from Satan. An evil man who hates and kills is demon-controlled. There are not three classes of people on the earth, only two, "the children of God . . . and the children of the devil" (1 John 3:10), and all murderers fall in the latter class. Cain who slew Abel, and the Jews who sought to kill Jesus, were Satan's children. Murder is not perpetrated under divine influence but under demonic influence.

Satan's urge to destroy human life prompted him to entice the first human to sin. God had placed one simple restriction on Adam and Eve. They were not to eat of the fruit of one tree, supported by God's warning, "for in the day that thou eatest thereof thou shalt surely die" (Genesis 2:17). But Satan, who is a liar from the beginning and a destroyer of the truth, said, "Ye shall not surely die" (Genesis 3:4). There was only one way in which Adam and Eve could sin, and that was to eat the forbidden fruit. So the liar and murderer set out to slay the first humans. The author of murder, his own heart set on killing, achieved his goal. Cain, the first human murderer, was of that wicked one. The chain has not been broken since that first killing.

The annual reports from the office of the Federal Bureau of Investigation have shown consistently an increase in crime. Murder is the most serious of all crimes. Every year thousands of innocent people, many of them mothers and fathers, are slain by demon-possessed killers. Satan is cruel, and to him life is cheap. His power over those who are his slaves is so strong they will kill anyone who resists their attempt to steal or rape. I have talked with murderers in prison who told me they were overcome by an irresistible urge to kill. It was a one-time urge, something they had never experienced before.

For five years I was appointed by the court to be the parole guardian for a convicted murderer. While in prison he received Jesus Christ as his Saviour and Lord. After he began studying the Bible he came to the conclusion that Satan took complete control of his mind and body the day he killed a man.

MURDER THE MONEYMAKER

The discovery and development of television is one of the scientific marvels of the twentieth century. I read the TV listings for one week and found murder in the following:

Our Man Flint: "His weapon, a simple cigarette lighter with 82 death-dealing devices."

Columbo: "The head of a think tank slays a fellow scientist."

Barnaby Jones: "A women's lib leader and female chauvinist writer have a public feud and a private affair that ends in the death of his wife."

Hawkins: "Hawkins is called to defend a movie star's husband in a Hollywood murder." In this one performance a sixteen-year-old girl was having a sexual affair with the man who was beaten to death with a golf club. The girl's mother was an alcoholic possessed of an uncontrolled sex drive for certain types of men. The murderer was a homosexual who had been involved with the murdered man. This satanic garbage was presented at 9:30 on a Tuesday night, an hour when millions of American youth were exposed to it.

Movie: "Murder in the Red Barn."

The Cowboys: "Slim sees a respected citizen kill a man."

Cannon: "A mercenary soldier obtains Cannon's services for a murder investigation."

Kung Fu: "Caine and a Texas lawman find themselves outside the law and accused of killing a man."

Murder is involved in the following television performances: *Mannix, The Streets of San Francisco, The Fearless Vampire Killers, The Untouchables, No Road Back, Hawaii Five-O.*

Every week television viewers witness between fifteen and twenty-five murders. I am convinced that satanic influence is behind the script writing of these performances, and I believe Satan uses all of this to feed the minds of youth with ideas that can make them killers. Yes, "all that is in the world [the world system]" (1 John 2:16) is a part of Satan's domain inasmuch as "the whole world [world system] lieth in wickedness" (1 John 5:19). The present sad and perilous state of the world proves that it is in the grip and dominion of Satan.

Some of my readers might accuse me of being fanatical about this, but such accusations only prove what the Bible teaches, namely the world "lieth"—quietly, unconsciously sleeping—in the arms of Satan. The inspired writer of Scripture does not blur the issue. We are either "of God" or of "the wicked one."

God is the Creator of life and Jesus came to give life. He said, "I am come that they might have life, and that they might have it more abundantly" (John 10:10). "And I give unto them eternal life; and they shall never perish, neither shall any man pluck them out of My hand" (John 10:28).

Satan's ambition is to destroy life. Jesus said, "The thief cometh not, but for to steal, and to kill, and to destroy" (John 10:10).

History shows that Satan is a murderer, and that he will continue to slaughter to the end. His followers are so thoroughly brain-washed as to believe that if they kill Christ's followers they are serving God (John 16:2). Read the account of the first recorded martyr and you will see Satan in action (Acts 7:54-58). The killing of James was looked upon by many Jews as a good thing (Acts 12:1-3). The god of this age, the evil murderer, can boast of having slain his millions. But the great tragedy lies in the fact that this demonic destroyer of life can control so many human beings to get them to carry out the crimes he planned.

Pharaoh was Satan's dupe when the Egyptian king ordered the Hebrew male babies to be slain (Exodus 1:22). *Athaliah,* daughter of the evil woman Jezebel, was Satan's puppet when she, in a moment of madness, plotted to destroy the royal messianic line (2 Kings 11:1-3). *Haman* was Satan's hatchet man when he schemed to wipe out the entire Hebrew race in one day (Esther 3:13). *Herod* was Satan's ace trigger man when he ordered the death of all innocent children two years old and under (Matthew 2:16). There are thousands of killers in prisons, and many more still free who have not been apprehended, who were inveigled into believing that life is cheap.

THE ABORTION ISSUE

"The War on the Womb" was the title of an editorial in *Christianity Today* (June 5, 1970). The title of that article indicated that the abortion issue had become a hot item for discussion in both the public and religious press. Christians and non-Christians have gotten into the forefront of the battle.

Should pregnant unwed girls and married women be free to dispose of an unborn baby at the whim of the expectant mother? Would laws preventing killing of the unborn, unwanted baby be an invasion of a woman's privacy? These are some of the questions raised by persons on both sides of the issue. And so the "war on the womb" waxes hotter and hotter.

Currently in the United States there are reportedly one million illegal abortions annually. The issue, reduced to simple terms, is this: Is the fetus a person having soul and spirit? Or is the fetus only a potential human life? The laws of the land cannot be based on the above questions, simply because there does not seem to be a clear-cut answer to them.

Dr. Kenneth M. Mitzner says, "By the time the presence of the baby can be verified, usually in the fourth week after conception, his heart is beating, the three principal regions of his brain have begun to differentiate, and all other organs are present in at least primitive form .... Abortion at six weeks kills a little human being with arms and legs, fingers and the beginning of toes ... at this age he will already respond, by flexing his neck and trunk ... at best, abortion is equivalent to killing a person in his sleep" ("The Growing Scandal of Abortion" *The Presbyterian Journal*, February 27, 1974).

What position should the Christian take on the issue? Certainly he cannot be persuaded by what the so-called "experts" say, nor by the women's liberation movement. When a Christian wants to know God's viewpoint on any matter, he must accept the Bible as God's Word and follow it as the basic standard. If we allow ourselves to be side-tracked by Satan's smoke screens, a true Biblical approach will be clouded.

I will not insist that the Bible speaks directly on abortion, but there are some principles in Scripture that apply to the ethics of abortion. Carl F. H. Henry said, "After all, abortion is not only of physical and legal interest, but equally a spiritual and moral concern" (*Baptist Herald,* March 1972). The life at stake is not the physician's, nor the mother's, nor the state's. The decision to preserve life or kill does not rest with parents. The unborn child has a right to life, a distinctive Christian principle. No mother has a right to kill her baby.

Premarital intercourse is a violation of God's holy command, "Thou shalt not commit adultery" (Exodus 20:14). An abortion to deliberately put to death an unwanted child conceived in sin only adds insult to injury, and it violates the commandment immediately preceding the above, "Thou shalt not kill" (Exodus 20:13). The Scriptures teach that the body is God's by creative right. That person in the womb is a truly living human. The will to kill does not originate with God, but with Satan.

I cannot find any Biblical basis for liberalizing abortion laws. I would not attempt to legislate ethics or morality for other people, but as a Christian I do not feel that the choice is every person's. Of course, there are complex physical and medical problems. There are those who sincerely believe and teach that it is better to abort than to bring a physically or mentally retarded child into the world. Again I must say that the decision to kill does not rest with the mother or the doctor. The issue is not a political or a social one; it is moral and spiritual.

Unless moral and spiritual values are restored, our civilization is in danger of further disintegration. Our teenagers are being hit from every angle—magazines, books, television, and even some laws, such as the liberal laws on abortion. God would not teach us to kill; Satan does.

LYING IS SATANIC

Our Lord said of Satan that he "abode not in the truth ... for he is a liar" (John 8:44). The first recorded lie in Scripture was spoken by Satan. God had said to our first parents, "But of the tree of the knowledge of good and evil, thou shalt not eat of it: for in the day that thou eatest thereof thou shalt surely die" (Genesis 2:17). Satan said to Eve, "Ye shall not surely die" (Genesis 3:4).

Actually Satan was accusing God of being a liar, that His word was not true and therefore He could not be trusted. What a wicked distortion of the truth! What clever subtlety! Convince a man that the Bible is not true, then he will believe your lie. Satan establishes this beachhead in the mind of every young child. The Bible says,"The wicked are estranged from the womb: they go astray as soon as they be born, speaking lies" (Psalm 58:3).

Every parent knows from experience that lying is one of the earliest overt sins committed by children. The Christians who know God's Word are not surprised when their children do not speak the truth. Every baby born into this world is a potential liar. No child ever has to be taught how to tell a lie. We all come into this world with a built-in crime system. We inherit this evil tendency from our parents

(Psalm 51:5; Romans 5:12), they inherited it from their parents, and so it is traced back to Satan's encounter with the first parents of the human race. The father of all untruth successfully invaded the human mind with this evil of lying. The leaven of lying arrives with us the day we appear. Adam's posterity comes into the world stained with the evil of deceit, therefore we cannot expect truth from one who is estranged from truth and righteousness. He who is "alienated from the life of God" (Ephesians 4:18) "is not subject to the law of God, neither indeed can be" (Romans 8:7). Paul's description of all unsaved persons is a vivid one. He says, "Their throat is an open sepulchre; with their tongues they have used deceit; the poison of asps is under their lips" (Romans 3:13).

Truth stands diametrically opposed to falsehood, to deceit. When God wrote laws for the children of Israel, He instructed them in their particular area of truthfulness saying, "Thou shalt not bear false witness against thy neighbour" (Exodus 20:16). This commandment demands sincerity and truth in man's relation to his fellowmen. A healthy relation between men is dependent upon truthfulness. Justice is based upon truth, therefore a false testimony produces a miscarriage of justice. For this reason perjury is considered a criminal offense in a court of human law. The slanderer who perpetrates a lie might destroy a good man's reputation beyond repair.

The sin of Ananias was influenced by Satan. Peter said, "Ananias, why hath Satan filled thine heart to lie to the Holy Ghost . . .?" (Acts 5:3)

The telling of the lie was voluntary on the part of Ananias, yet it was prompted by the devil, the first liar and the father of all lies. The devil suggested that he cheat by lying. Ananias could have resisted him (James 4:7). When any man seeks to gain a higher reputation than he deserves, and that by deceit, he is being led astray by his adversary the devil.

A false witness can be given by means of the subtle form of insinuation. This is frequently done by the question method. For example, some rumors were afloat about the behavior of a certain minister in Pennsylvania. A pastor approached me with the question, "Did you hear about ————— and his problem?" I told him I had not heard anything about the brother. To my answer he responded with, "Oh, well, the least said about it the better." There was no accusation made that would have to be proved later, but there was the devilish insinuation that my friend had been involved in something that was wrong. Such an approach is a satanic evil.

Satan asked God, "Doth Job fear God for nought?" (Job 1:9) Satan did not accuse Job of any wrong, but behind his question was a wicked inference which was nothing less than outright deceit. All liars are satanically influenced, therefore "all liars shall have their part in the lake which burneth with fire and brimstone" (Revelation 21:8). Liars choose to follow the devil, therefore they must spend eternity with him, for "the devil that deceived them" will be "cast into the lake of fire and brimstone" (Revelation 20:10). It is not incidental when the Bible says that murderers, liars, and Satan will share a common fate throughout eternity.

THERE IS HOPE FOR MURDERERS AND LIARS

Even though Satan and his demons will continue to make murderers and liars of men and women until the final exorcism, there is hope for any person to be spared from becoming one of Satan's killers. God said to His people, "Thou shalt not kill" (Exodus 20:13). Satan put the seed of murder in the mind of Moses, and Moses yielded to the temptation and slew an Egyptian (Exodus 2:11-14). The details in the narrative reveal that Moses knew he did wrong. That murder was a victory for Satan. A life was prematurely cut off.

Satan made it convenient for David to murder Uriah, the Hittite, and David followed the evil suggestion (2 Samuel 11). "But the thing that David had done displeased the LORD" (2 Samuel 11:27). True, both Moses and David, along with many since their time, repented and were forgiven by God, but think of the many murders that would have been prevented if only the killers had discovered the power of prevention.

There is one power greater than that of Satan—the power of God. One of the purposes of the Incarnation (God becoming man) was to restrain Satan's power over man to make him want to kill. "Forasmuch then as the children are partakers of flesh and blood, He also Himself likewise took part of the same; that through death He might destroy him that had the power of death, that is, the devil" (Hebrews 2:14).

God the eternal Son, who existed in spirit form, took on Him a human body (became incarnate) in order that He might "destroy" (Greek, *katargeo*) i.e., render inactive, Satan's strong power over death. The word translated "destroy" is in the Revised Version rendered "bring to nought." It means "to deprive of influence and power." To bring to naught the devil does not have reference to depriving him of further existence, but to depriving him of power to hold men under death. This power is not a dominion formally given to him, but rather a power that he has to cause man to sin, a sinning which results in death (Genesis 2:17; Ezekiel 18:4; Romans 5:12,14; 6:23; James 1:15). When sin entered, death entered. And as long as Satan prevails to keep men in their sins, he has the power to keep them under the sentence and fear of death.

Men and women are creatures of flesh and blood, the very life Satan seeks to destroy. Therefore Christ became a partaker of flesh and blood in order that He should die, and in the very act of dying wrest the keys of death and Hades from Satan. Another New Testament passage says, "For this purpose the Son of God was manifested, that He might destroy the works of the devil" (1 John 3:8).

The particular work of the devil is sin, and sin and death are inseparably linked together; therefore one of the purposes of the Son of God's appearing is to rescue man from sin and death. By laying down His life, and rising from death and the grave, Christ overcame the death of which the devil has power. The devil knows that the law of God demands death for sin, and even though he is a liar and a deceiver, there is justice in his claim that the sinner must die. He has the power and authority to insist that every sinner die.

Through His death on the cross and His resurrection, Christ gives new life. It is true that our bodies of flesh and blood are still mortal and corruptible, and as such must die. However, the fear and sting of death are gone the moment the believing sinner receives new life in Christ (1 Corinthians 15:53-57). Jesus said, "The thief cometh not, but for to steal, and to kill, and to destroy: I am come that they might have life, and that they might have it more abundantly. I am the good shepherd: the good shepherd giveth His life for the sheep" (John 10:10-11).

Today Jesus sits at God's right hand, "crowned with glory and honour." He became man, "that He by the grace of God should taste death for every man" (Hebrews 2:9). Because Christ suffered, and because His suffering has been crowned by His resurrection, ascension, and exaltation, therefore His death avails for all mankind. "I am He that liveth, and was dead; and, behold, I am alive for evermore, Amen; and have the keys of hell and of death" (Revelation 1:18).

It was all "by the grace of God," by His free, immeasurable kindness that sinners should be released from death and should inherit eternal life. Satan's hold upon man could be broken only by the removal of the sin that results in death. Christ's death was God's righteous judgment of sin. Satan had nothing whatever to do with it. The transaction was settled in Heaven when the Father and the Son agreed that the iniquity of us all should be laid on the Son (Isaiah 53:6). It is not by His life, nor by His example, nor by His teachings that Christ delivers us from Satan's power, but by His death which removes sin with its guilt and power. Now those who are Christ's are free, and Satan has no claim upon the children of God. Nothing but disobedience and unbelief can keep men in bondage to Satan. The Christian's evil enemy can hinder and assault us, but he can never take from us the life that we have in Christ. We have passed "from death unto life" (John 5:24). "We know that we have passed from death unto life, because we love the brethren. He that loveth not his brother abideth in death. Whosoever hateth his brother is a murderer: and ye know that no murderer hath eternal life abiding in him" (1 John 3:14-15).

The morality of Christianity is based upon the positive teachings in the Word of God. But we are living in a generation when men have jettisoned the Bible as an authoritative guide for moral behavior. Those who tell us that our society can get along perfectly well without the Biblical standards of morality have substituted their "new morality" which is nothing less than immorality. When men abandon the laws of God which control human behavior, the only other force to control their conduct is the power of Satan.

SATAN'S ECUMENICAL CHURCH

On April 30, 1966 Auton Szandor La Vey announced the formation of the Church of Satan in the city of San Francisco. Today there are reportedly thousands of carefully screened, dues-paying members. This makes La Vey's Church of Satan the fastest growing church in America. Auton La Vey wrote a book which he titled, *The Satanic Bible,* the guide book for his followers. This religion occupies the same place in the lives of La Vey's followers that all other religions normally occupy in their members.

La Vey's Church of Satan might appear to many to be a bold, shocking thing. Actually it is only a public show of something that has been going on in men's hearts for thousands of years. The Church of Satan was not founded by Auton La Vey but by Satan himself. It just so happens that our deteriorating culture has in recent years created a new and growing interest in the occult, which is supposed to contain hidden secrets about the future. Clairvoyance, transcendental meditation, astrology, psychicism, spiritism, out-of-body trips, and other forms of mysticism are attracting many new converts to Satan's church. What is going on in the occult world today is new to most Americans, but it is nothing more than the supernatural practices that have found expression in more ancient cultures.

Supernatural forces are presently making swift headway into the religious life of America. Satan and his demons are planting ideas in the minds of millions of Americans. Many religious publishing companies are aiding and promoting the devil's religion. From the Atlantic to the Pacific, from Canada to the Gulf of Mexico, everywhere in our nation, Satan's ecumenical church is spreading. Satan is not only alive and active, he is being worshiped openly both knowingly and ignorantly. He confronts the religionist and the moralist. His church is flourishing.

I am convinced that the majority of people today who are involved with Satan's church, are not aware of the fact that they are in league with man's greatest enemy. Should our Lord not return within the lifetime of our generation, I predict that Satan and his religion will capture millions more. The professing church of the twentieth century will not openly admit to satanic forces being active in the religious life of the western world, but this blindness is the result of the low level of spiritual life and a departure from the Bible as God's authoritative word to man.

RELIGION IS SATAN'S STOCK IN TRADE

The dramatic revolt of Lucifer had definite religious overtones. He said, "I will be like the most High" (Isaiah 14:14). But why would he try to be like God? The answer is obvious. He is seeking both men and angels to worship him. Man is intuitively and instinctively religious, having been created with God-consciousness. Satan's desire to be like God has forever set the pattern of his activities. The whole satanic world system is organized in its united effort to win men over to Satan-worship.

Satan's ambition to be worshiped reached the peak of blasphemy when he said to Jesus, "All these things will I give Thee, if Thou wilt fall down and *worship* me" (Matthew 4:9).

If we want to know the devil's main goal, we will find it in this text in the word "worship." Involved in worship is the idea of service. The one we worship is the one we serve and obey. Had Jesus bowed the knee and worshiped Satan, He would have become Satan's slave. Of course, we know Jesus could not have bowed to Satan. But man, who is so constituted that he is made to worship, will worship and serve God or Satan. And be certain, Satan is having his big day in persuading men to worship and serve him. This, more than anything else, is what Satan wants from you and me.

Satan is inaugurating a worldwide system of religion that will culminate in that "man of sin," the man over whom Satan will have absolute control. Some able scholars believe that this "man of sin" will be the devil incarnate, the Antichrist, the "seed" of the serpent (Genesis 3:15). Paul describes him as the one "Who opposeth and exalteth himself above all that is called God, or that is worshipped; so that he as God sitteth in the temple of God, shewing himself that he is God" (2 Thessalonians 2:4). If he is the Antichrist, he will claim absolute and exclusive deity, wanting to be worshiped by all men as God. Nothing has appeared in history which answers to Paul's description. As evil approaches its height, it will assume more and more a religious character. Claiming deity is the crowning wickedness of Satan.

Read carefully Revelation 13. The details correspond to those in 2 Thessalonians 2:4. It is a tribulation scene. Of the earth's population in that day, John writes, "And they *worshipped* the dragon" (Revelation 13:4), who is Satan (12:9). Christ's true Church will have been caught up to be with Him, so all that remains on earth of a religious nature will be in Satan's ecumenical church, whose influence will extend to the whole inhabited earth. John continues, "And all that dwell upon the earth shall *worship* him, whose names are not written in the book of life of the Lamb slain from the foundation of the world" (Revelation 13:8). Satan will be so demanding at that time that any who refuse to worship him will do so under penalty of death (13:15). I believe we are witnessing today the setting of the stage, which is the preparation for the fulfillment of this amazing prophecy.

The growing effort to unite all churches into one world church is Satan's plan. It is his ecumenical church. The word "ecumenical" comes to us from the Greek word *oikoumene*, which in its root meaning denotes "the inhabited earth." In the New Testament it is sometimes translated "all the world" (Matthew 24:14; Luke 2:1). For many years liberal theologians have been advocating an organic union between church groups even though they differ widely in belief and practice. This ecumenical ferment is gaining momentum, and for Protestantism the World Council of Churches has become its voice. I personally believe that the World Council of Churches is playing into the hands of Satan and that it will play a more significant part in the devil's church in the end times.

SATAN'S MESSAGE AND METHOD

Satan exercises influence over all unsaved people (John 8:44; 1 John 5:19). Paul reminds us Christians that, before we were saved, we too, "walked according to the course of this world, according to the prince of the power of the air, the spirit that now worketh in the children of disobedience" (Ephesians 2:2). But in order to hold the unbeliever captive, Satan has devised both a message and a method to accomplish this.

The message of Satan is an imitation of the gospel of Christ. Paul warned the Galatians: "I marvel that ye are so soon removed from Him that called you into the grace of Christ into another gospel: Which is not another; but there be some that trouble you, and would pervert the gospel of Christ. But though we, or an angel from heaven, preach any other gospel unto you than that which we have preached unto you, let him be accursed" (Galatians 1:6-9). You see, there are many gospels. Paul preached "the gospel of Christ" (Romans 1:16), which is the message of Christ's substitutionary death, burial, and resurrection for sinners (1 Corinthians 15:1-4). But he warned the churches in Galatia, that they should be on the watch for "another gospel," that is, *another of a different kind.* Satan has his ministers, called "false apostles, deceitful workers, transforming themselves into the apostles of Christ" (2 Corinthians 11:13). The Holy Spirit had enlightened Paul as to the devices of Satan, thus Paul knew how the enemy would imitate both the message and messenger of the pure gospel.

There are numerous spurious gospels, the latest in our time being the "social gospel." The devil would have men believe that the church's responsibility is to minister to the social needs of people. Now the social gospel is not all bad, but it is powerless to deliver men from the guilt and penalty of sin. It is counterfeit.

There is a sure way to test the devil's preachers and their preaching. The Apostle John wrote, "Beloved, believe not every spirit, but try the spirits whether they are of God: because many false prophets are gone out into the world. Hereby know ye the Spirit of God: Every spirit that confesseth that Jesus Christ is come in the flesh is of God: And every spirit that confesseth not that Jesus Christ is come in the flesh is not of God: and this is that spirit of antichrist, whereof ye have heard that it should come; and even now already is it in the world" (1 John 4:1-3). The devil's preachers deny the deity, substitutionary death, and bodily resurrection of our Lord Jesus Christ. Therefore we are warned against those who preach "another Jesus" and "another gospel" by "another spirit" (2 Corinthians 11:4).

In 1 John 2:22 we read, "Who is a liar but he that denieth that Jesus is the Christ? He is antichrist, that denieth the Father and the Son." The satanic system that has its ministers in the world is presenting "another Jesus," not the Jesus of the Bible. The terms, "another Jesus" (2 Corinthians 11:4) and "false Christs" (Matthew 24:5, 24), have taken on new meaning in the past fifteen years. Many new movements have been born which use the name of Jesus. The "Jesus Revolution" is upon us, but don't be misled by that name Jesus. Some movements and musicians are using Jesus as a frame of reference to lure the unwary into Satan's sieve. Some promoters will use people and gimmicks in order to get a crowd and "lift" an offering, but reverence for the holy name is conspicuous by its absence.

Satan's bold stroke in counterfeiting the Christ of the Bible was introduced with the rock opera, *Jesus Christ, Superstar.* Every student of the Bible who has examined the lyrics of *Superstar* knows that its Christ is Satan's Christ, not the Christ of the Scriptures. "Another Jesus" has captured the attention of young people.

One of the hottest items in show business today is "rock and roll music." Rock groups (some of them) make more money in one year than the highest paid sports stars and business executives. Brian Epstein, mastermind of the Beatles, "earned $14 million in five years," according to a *London Times* report. Brian Epstein was found dead at age 32 from "the cumulative effect of a bromide in a drug he had been taking for some time." His Beatles boasted that the quartet was more popular than Jesus Christ. It was the style and success of the Beatles that inspired two young Englishmen to produce Satan's Christ in their blasphemous *Jesus Christ, Superstar.* There are congregations today, Roman Catholic and Protestant, who have introduced the music of *Jesus Christ, Superstar* into their worship services. Some of this kind of music is attended by evil effects upon the human soul and spirit. It is jungle tribalism in a new dress, a part of Satan's religion. Young people, beware of the numerous movements which have adopted the name "Jesus." You could be swaying and clapping your hands to Satan's music. There could be many people in churches today who actually worship Satan while believing they are worshiping God.

I am not passing judgment on all of the new groups with a "Jesus" message. God is the final Judge. But many sensible saints are disturbed and concerned about some of the self-styled, flashy combo groups who move from church to church with a new dress and a new beat that has no serious and reverent sense of God.

Dr. Vance Havner said, "One does not think of translating Shakespeare into hillbilly vernacular, or reducing Beethoven to rock-'n'-roll. The idea that we must imitate the world in clothes, language, and music to make the gospel attractive is not divine but demonic. To begin with, the gospel was never meant for entertainment. The sin against the Holy Spirit lay in ascribing the work of God to the devil. Is it not equally possible to ascribe the work of the devil to God? I do not believe that spiritually sensitive souls can equate gospel jazz and hippie hootenannies with the hallelujahs of the redeemed" (*Not Peace But A Sword*, page 38).

Satan is adept in the art of deception. He is cunning enough to know that if he can disguise his Christ to appear like the Christ of the Bible, he will keep men from accepting the saving message of Christ's gospel. Satan's religion is the counterfeit of God's salvation for sinners. I have had the privilege of speaking in more than 1,100 different churches in America, and I have been shocked and grieved over the lack of discernment in many professing Christians. I have seen demonic powers at work, blinding the minds of young and older persons alike as to the pure gospel of grace. Demonic perversions of the gospel are appearing more frequently now than at any time during the past fifty years.

While ministering in a church in New Jersey I was confronted by a young man, a professing Christian, who was just starting to become involved in the charismatic cult. He defended the movement by telling me its leaders believed the gospel. When I asked him to define the Christian gospel, he did not have the faintest idea where to begin. The gospel is absolutely and totally different from every religion in the world, and it is sufficient to save a sinner for time and eternity. Satanic perversions are introduced the moment anything is added to, or taken from, Christ's substitutionary death and bodily resurrection from death and the grave. If demonic powers are unsuccessful in keeping men away from the gospel altogether, then they will present "another Jesus" and "another gospel," which is in reality no gospel at all.

A "Jesus" who is not both Christ and Lord is "another Jesus." The Bible says, "Believe on the *Lord Jesus Christ,* and thou shalt be saved, and thy house" (Acts 16:31). "That if thou shalt confess with thy mouth the *Lord Jesus,* and shalt believe in thine heart that God hath raised Him from the dead, thou shalt be saved" (Romans 10:9).

An evil spirit once said, "*Jesus* I know" (Acts 19:15), but "no man can say that *Jesus is* Lord, but by the Holy Ghost" (1 Corinthians 12:3). I like to hear a child of God witness reverently and humbly to faith in, and submission to, the *Lord Jesus Christ.*

SATAN PERFORMS MIRACLES

One of Satan's most insidious and successful devices to deceive is in the area of miracles. Harry Houdini was an artful deceiver in the art of deception, but everyone knew that he performed tricks. But Satan is not a professional magician. This enemy of God and man possesses supernatural power.

The Lord Jesus spoke an amazing prophecy of the end times. He said, "For there shall arise false Christs, and false prophets, and shall shew great signs [miracles] and wonders; insomuch that, if it were possible, they shall deceive the very elect" (Matthew 24:24). If I did not have this word from Jesus Himself, I might hesitate to venture into this discussion. But with my Bible open before me, I will proceed.

In Moses' day God told Aaron and Moses that Pharaoh would ask them to "shew [perform] a miracle" (Exodus 7:9). Human nature has not changed since the time of Pharaoh. It was this desire for the miraculous and spectacular that led Nicodemus to Jesus (compare John 3:2 with 2:11,23).

God told Moses and Aaron what they were to do when Pharaoh asked for a miracle. Aaron was to cast his rod to the ground before Pharaoh, and it would immediately become a crawling snake (Exodus 7:9). This would indeed be a miracle. Aaron obeyed, and God performed the miracle before Pharaoh's eyes (7:10).

Immediately upon seeing the miracle, Pharaoh called for his sorcerers and magicians who duplicated the miracle of God (7:11-12). Egyptian magic and sorcery was simply the calling of evil spirits for the purpose of divining. The word "sorcerer" or "sorceress" is the correct rendering of the term "witch," used twice in the Old Testament, in Exodus 22:18 and Deuteronomy 18:10 (see the Revised Version). The witch or sorcerer uses occult formulas and incantations to summon demonic powers. Similiar satanic miracles were repeated in Exodus 7:22; 8:6-7,16-18. Of course, Satan performed those miracles by God's permissive will, but the fact remains that he did them. Satan had a most convincing argument to hold those Egyptians in bondage. To them the occult was the great power. Their performance was no mere sleight of hand, but real feats of evil supernaturalism. Such miraculous demonstrations of demon power occur periodically, usually when there is a genuine spiritual awakening in progress. In the midst of the revival in Samaria Satan had his man ready to counterfeit the miracles of God. The crowds gathered to hear Philip preach Christ and see the miracles that accompanied his preaching (Acts 8:5-8). Then without any break in the narrative, Luke continues, "But there was a certain man, called Simon, which beforetime in the same city used sorcery, and bewitched the people of Samaria, giving out that himself was some great one: To whom they all gave heed, from the least to the greatest, saying, This man is the great power of God" (Acts 8:9-10). Here was a demon-possessed man who, through sorcery, performed such great miracles that people mistook him for the true agent of God.

God is working miracles today, but so also is Satan. As people become increasingly disillusioned by the dead orthodoxy and liberal apostasy in so many churches, they are easy prey for Satan's counterfeit. Gideon asked God, in a time of spiritual declension in Israel, "Oh my Lord, if the LORD be with us, why then is all this befallen us? and where be all His miracles which our fathers told us of . . . ?" (Judges 6:13)

Today people are asking, Where are the miracles? In my travels across America I hear a lot of loose talk about miracles. One popular "faith healer" reminds his television viewers to "expect a miracle today." Another religious leader conducts his "miracle ranch" in western United States. Many people are looking for some supernatural phenomenon, an event quite distinct from the laws of nature. There is today in religious circles a flare for the miraculous, the spectacular, the demonstrative. Crowds gather where miracles are promised.

SATAN'S HEALING PROGRAM

When I was ministering at a prophetic conference in California, a lady shared with me a most informative testimony. In her earlier years she lived in Detroit, Michigan, and was an active member in the Christian Science Church. She suffered from severe head pains, and for many months she kept her suffering a secret, knowing that her Christian Science friends and relatives would not accept the fact of sickness. When she could no longer bear the pain, she sought the help of a physician who persuaded her to enter Grace Hospital in Detroit for X-rays and tests. She agreed to do this against the advice of family and friends. A team of doctors studied her carefully and concluded that she had a brain tumor which called for immediate surgery. She told me she would have submitted to the surgery, but her family pressured her into leaving the hospital and going to a Christian Science practitioner for healing. Upon her first visit to the Christian Science practitioner she was healed instantly. A subsequent examination by the same physicians at Grace Hospital showed no signs whatever of the tumor. She had been healed.

However, as time went on she became bothered by the fact that, one by one, her Christian Science friends and loved ones became sick and died. This disturbed her greatly. She concluded that one day she too would be stricken with her last illness that would result in death. But what about after

death? Where would she spend eternity? Fearing death and
what lay beyond, she made an appointment with Dr. William
Coltman, then pastor of the Highland Park Baptist Church.
She unburdened her heart to that godly pastor, whereupon
he opened his Bible, and step by step showed her from God's
Word that all are sinners and in need of God's salvation made
available in Jesus Christ. That day she received Christ and
was saved from the guilt and penalty of her sins.

Without any human prompting, that woman saw at
once that the devil had healed her body temporarily so that
he might hold her soul in bondage to share eternity with
him in the lake of fire.

Can Satan heal? You better believe he can! He does
perform miracles, including bodily healing. He can operate
through any present-day healing movement. His miracles
add credence to his false teaching, which in turn gains followers. I personally pray for discernment lest I accept too
easily and rejoice too quickly in the reports of miracles. I
believe in divine healing, and by that I am saying that I believe
God can and does heal supernaturally. But I am convinced
that not all miracles of healing are performed by God.

Mediumistic healers are prevalent in all parts of the
world. Let me explain what I mean by *mediumistic.* I believe
the word comes to us from the Latin word *medium,* meaning
middle, intermediary. A medium is a person who is the go-
between where there are two or more unseen forces. A spir-
itist medium mediates between invisible spirits. There are
people who are mediumistically inclined and who seem to have
the ability to contact spirit forces.

I find very few Christians with any knowledge about
spirit mediums. Because of this ignorance the average Christian cannot discern between divine healing and mediumistic
healing. Mediumistic powers are satanic, therefore they are
dangerous even when healing bodies of the sick.

Mrs. Strauss and I became acquainted with a doctor in Fort Collins, Colorado. He heard of an "astral surgeon" in the Philippines who operated on bodies of people without the use of any instrument. By merely manipulating his hands he diagnosed the illness, and proceeded to open the flesh and remove the diseased part. Our doctor friend visited the healer and was granted permission to take motion pictures of such an operation on a woman patient. My wife and I viewed the entire procedure on film. There were no surgical instruments, no attendants, no medication, and no sewing together of the incision. We saw the incision being made with the manipulation of the hands of the "surgeon," and the diseased organ removed. The healer was guided by an unseen force to the trouble spot inside the patient's body. There was a flow of blood. In a few minutes the entire operation was completed, and the patient stood up and walked to her house a healed person. That is a case of mediumistic healing. The healer was not a Christian. He depended solely on a clairvoyant diagnosis and healing. He received his power from evil spirits.

To argue that modern healers attract great crowds and collect large sums of money is no proof that their gift of healing has come from God. Since when was the devil poor? When are his places of business lacking for customers? Modern healers who ply their trade by preying upon the sick never received their gift from the Holy Spirit. The healings being witnessed today are largely the work of evil spirits masquerading under the guise of faith healing. A sound Christian faith built upon the knowledge of God's Word will provide discernment for the child of God.

Christian, be on your guard! Don't expect to find Satan in a house of prostitution, or in an adult movie house, or in a gambler's den. You will find him more often in a pulpit where he has his minister (2 Corinthians 11:13), teaching doctrines of demons (1 Timothy 4:1), even the deep things of Satan (Revelation 2:24). Satan has a doctrine to spread and a method of making it known. He will often put on a demonstration of miracles. Satan's avowed purpose to control the thinking of men is making progress through "evil men and seducers" (2 Timothy 3:13). Satan is in the business of religion, and his goal is to capture and control as many religious people as possible.

THE SINISTER SATAN—MAN

"And without controversy great is the mystery of godliness: God was manifest in the flesh, justified in the Spirit, seen of angels, preached unto the [nations], believed on in the world, received up into glory" (1 Timothy 3:16).

"For the mystery of iniquity doth already work: only he who now hindereth will continue to hinder until he be taken out of the way" (2 Thessalonians 2:7).

These two verses of Scripture have something in common. Both mention a "mystery" (Greek, *musterion*). Now a mystery in the Bible is not something that is mysterious. The word is generally misunderstood. Among the Greeks the "mystery" was a rite or ceremony known and practiced only by those persons who had been initiated into the secret society. Nonmembers did not know those secrets. Once a new member was officially received into the organization or society, the mystery (or secret) was made known, so that the aura of mystery was no longer there. A mystery suggests that knowledge is withheld from certain people.

Not less than eleven mysteries are mentioned in the Bible. These are secret truths that God had withheld until He revealed them to His people in His time. These holy secrets are beyond the apprehension and comprehension of the natural mind, because "the natural man receiveth not the things of the Spirit of God: for they are foolishness unto him: neither can he know them, because they

57

are spiritually discerned" (1 Corinthians 2:14). The "natural man" is the unsaved man "In whom the god of this world [Satan] hath blinded the minds of them which believe not" (2 Corinthians 4:4), "having [their] understanding darkened" (Ephesians 4:18).

When the believing sinner receives the Lord Jesus Christ he is born again into God's family and thereby becomes one of the initiated (Greek, *mustes*). It is to His own that God reveals His great hidden secrets. This tremendous body of New Testament teaching known as "mysteries" was kept secret for at least four thousand years of human history. The idea is best explained and illustrated in the following passage: "Even the mystery which hath been hid from ages and from generations, but now is made manifest to His saints" (Colossians 1:26).

These hidden secrets are called by the Lord Jesus Christ "the mysteries of the kingdom of heaven" (Matthew 13:11). He said, "I will utter things which have been kept *secret* from the foundation of the world" (Matthew 13:35). Jesus disclosed the first of the hidden secrets in His parables in Matthew 13. But even then He did not tell all. He said to His disciples, "I have yet many things to say unto you, but ye cannot bear them now. [Nevertheless] when He, the Spirit of truth, is come, He will guide you into all truth: for He shall not speak of Himself, but [whatever] He shall hear, that shall He speak: and He will shew you things to come" (John 16:12-13).

The further revelation of the mysteries was given to the Apostle Paul, two of those secrets being "the mystery of godliness" and "the mystery of iniquity." They represent two spheres of supernaturalism working on the earth today. Both mysteries refer to a person, and both persons are the incarnation of spirit beings. They are the two "seeds" mentioned in the first overt prophecy in the Bible. After the fall of Adam and Eve, God said to Satan, "And I will put enmity between thee and the woman, and between thy seed and her seed; [He] shall bruise thy head, and thou shalt bruise His heel" (Genesis 3:15).

"Thy seed" and "her seed" represent Satan's man and God's man. The "seed" of the serpent is "the man of sin . . . the son of perdition" (2 Thessalonians 2:3). The "seed" of the woman is God's Son "made of a woman" (Galatians 4:4, compare 3:16). God determined that there should be "enmity" (war) between the seeds. The conflict would end when the woman's Seed, the God-Man, Jesus Christ, crushes Satan's head. And now for some six thousand years the conflict has been raging. Satan and his demons have continued to pursue the destruction of man. Paul said, "The mystery of iniquity doth already work" (2 Thessalonians 2:7).

THE PEOPLE OF THE SEEDS

The conflict between good and evil, between Christ and Satan, is reflected in the people of the seeds. God has His children who become such through receiving Christ (John 1:12; Galatians 3:26), and the devil has his seed who choose to follow him (John 8:44). Satan is at all times the aggressor in his determination to destroy the children of God. He knows his fate is sealed as already pronounced by God, and he was the first to hear it. Both seeds were to suffer, but Christ would finally and fatally wound Satan. In Genesis 3:15 there is both the prophetic and symbolic reference to Christ and His cross, where man would be redeemed and Satan repressed.

Murder was the first method employed by Satan in his attempt to destroy the good seed. He struck in the very first generation from our first parents, in the persons of their two sons, Cain and Abel. Here the two "seeds" come clearly into view. Cain and Abel were both taught to worship God in the same way, at the same time and place, and both learned from their parents that God required a sacrifice (Hebrews 11:4, compare 9:22). When God rejected Cain's offering, he became violent and murdered his brother (Genesis 4:8). What prompted him to kill his brother? God said he did it because he "was of that wicked one" (1 John 3:12).

God Himself had aroused the enmity between the two seeds and their kin, a good and holy enmity on the part of God's children against the evil wiles of the enemy. Such enmity against sin and Satan is a virtue. So when Abel resisted the temptations of Satan, the same temptations used to capture Cain, Satan put it in Cain's heart to slay his brother. That was merely the first skirmish in the battle of the seeds, and though Satan emerged a victor, God had already predicted his final overthrow. But Cain "missed the mark," the meaning of the word "sin," here mentioned for the first time in Scripture (Genesis 4:7). Cain's sin of hostility and murder was induced by Satan.

But God had pronounced the final outcome of the battle. *First*, He punished the murderer (Genesis 4:10-12), teaching him, and us, that human blood (human life) is precious, and that the fate of all murderers is certain. *Secondly*, another son was born to Adam and Eve, an act whereby is seen the gracious hand of God. Adam and Eve knew this because this son, Seth by name, was a gift from God in place of Abel. It is clear that God intended Seth to be a substitute for Abel. Later, after Seth married, a son was born, named Enos. Thus the godly line, the seed of the woman, continued, for we read, "Then began men to call upon the name of the LORD" (Genesis 4:26). This all bears eloquent testimony to the fact that God's pronouncement upon Satan was not to be thwarted. Satan sought to strike God through Cain, but

God is almighty and cannot be defeated.

Mixture was the next method employed by Satan in the conflict between the people of the seeds. Sin, which began with an individual, then a family, then spread its ugliness into the whole of society. The seed of the serpent now invaded the society of the seed of the woman. Satan concluded that since he could not win with *murder*, he would resort to *mixture*. In Genesis 6 we have the commingling of the two seeds, an unholy alliance between the Sethites (God's children) and the Cainites (Satan's children). The unequal yoke between believers and unbelievers is forbidden by God (2 Corinthians 6:14). God had drawn early the line of demarcation in Genesis 4:26.

The Cainites and the Sethites were the two streams of mankind in the human race, the two seeds, strictly kept apart because they were so utterly different in practice and purpose. Men like Enoch walked with God (Genesis 5:22). But then there were those of the godly line who were attracted by pretty faces and shapely bodies, some of whom were of the godless line, Satan's seed. The appalling results of this unholy alliance are summed up in the following terribly descriptive terms: "And God saw that the wickedness of man was great in the earth, and that every imagination of the thoughts of his heart was only evil continually .... The earth also was corrupt before God, and the earth was filled with violence. And God looked upon the earth, and, behold, it was corrupt; for all flesh had corrupted his way upon the earth. And God said unto Noah, The end of all flesh is come before Me; for the earth is filled with violence through them; and, behold, I will destroy them with the earth" (Genesis 6:5,11-13).

God was not taken by surprise. He witnessed the growing apostasy and the resulting demoralizing of the human race. However, not all of the good seed apostatized. Had all followed Satan, and been destroyed by the flood, the history of man would have ended, and the promise in Genesis 3:15 would have failed with Satan emerging the winner. But God had one man whom He could trust, Noah, a man of faith, courage, and piety (Hebrews 11:7; 2 Peter 2:5). The godly "Noah found grace in the eyes of the LORD" (Genesis 6:8). So despite the deadly commingling of good and bad, God had His man whom He could trust and use. And so the good seed was spared.

Let us turn to Matthew 13 for a brief look at our Lord's mystery parables. The second of these parables is often referred to as the parable of the tares (Matthew 13:24-30). Keep in mind that our Lord is revealing for the first time a mystery, a secret which had been hidden in the counsels of God from past ages. He is discussing something new, the kingdom in mystery, covering that period from His rejection and death to His future return to the earth to take the kingdom to which He holds the title deed. During His absence, the period including the present church era, there would be wheat and tares (true and false professors). In the present economy there is always present the element of evil mixed with the good.

Jesus said, "The good seed are the children of the kingdom; but the tares are the children of the wicked one; The enemy that sowed them is the devil; the harvest is the end of the world [age]; and the reapers are the angels" (Matthew 13:38-39). The startling feature of this parable is its description of Satan's strategy to cause his seed to appear like the children of God. This is Satan's masterpiece of deception. The mystery of iniquity is made to look like the mystery of godliness, but Satan's counterfeit is exposed as "Having a form of godliness, but denying the power thereof: from such turn away" (2 Timothy 3:5).

What is the real difference between the mystery of godliness and the mystery of iniquity? Let us examine each.

THE MYSTERY OF GODLINESS

We recall that Lucifer said, "I will be *like* the most High" (Isaiah 14:14), and that he said to Eve, "Ye shall be *as* gods" (Elohim, meaning God). Satan's ministers are "transformed *as* the ministers of righteousness" (2 Corinthians 11:15). Note those words "like" and "as." Neither Satan nor man can become God. At best the master deceiver can produce a mere likeness. The tares might look like the wheat, but they are not the same. False doctrine can be mixed with pure doctrine, but the two are markedly different (Matthew 13:33). God is eternal and self-existent; men and angels are His creation.

"God is . . . Spirit" (John 4:24), and "a spirit hath not flesh and bones" (Luke 24:39). The "mystery" (secret) not revealed in Genesis 3:15 is that God Himself, in the Person of His Son, would be the woman's Seed. "The mystery of godliness" is the fact of the Incarnation, that God Himself would take upon Him a human body in the Person of Jesus Christ. John wrote, "The Word was God . . . . And the Word was made [became] flesh" (John 1:1,14). "God was in Christ, reconciling the world unto Himself" (2 Corinthians 5:19). Jesus said, "He that hath seen Me hath seen the Father" (John 14:9). "I and My Father are one" (John 10:30). Jesus is God come to earth. He is the seed of the woman who will ultimately crush the seed of the serpent. The purpose of the Incarnation, then, is that God, through Christ, will strike the fatal blow to Satan and his kingdom and restore the universe to Jesus Christ, the God-Man, and subject it to Him. "That in the dispensation of the fulness of times He might gather together in one all things in Christ, both which are in heaven, and which are on earth; even in Him" (Ephesians 1:10).

Then "the mystery of God should [shall] be finished, as He hath declared to His servants the prophets" (Revelation 10:7). This mystery, like all Bible mysteries, is made known by divine revelation, and it assures the child of God of the glorious prospect of future conquest over all evil. "Forasmuch then as the children are partakers of flesh and blood, He also Himself likewise took part of the same; that through death He might destroy him that had the power of death, that is, the devil" (Hebrews 2:14). "For this purpose the Son of God was manifested, that He might destroy the works of the devil" (1 John 3:8).

The mystery of godliness, namely the Incarnation of the eternal Son of God, is the one fact, above all others, the devil hates, simply because it foretells his doom. Little wonder Satan's strategy is aimed at this precious truth. The special characteristic of the end-time apostasy will be Satan's all-out fight to draw people away from the truth of Christ's deity. Satan's counter movement is the mystery of iniquity, and "some are already turned aside after Satan" (1 Timothy 5:15).

The devil is possessed of a diabolical hatred for Christ and His Church, especially for those servants of Christ like Paul who emphasized in his teaching the mystery of godliness. There are numerous incidents recorded in Scripture of Paul having suffered severely at Satan's hands merely because he revealed these secrets given to him by God. The story of Paul's imprisonment furnishes us with a pattern of satanic opposition to the truth of the Incarnation. When Paul wrote the classic exposing the devil's wiles and the believer's defensive weapons, he urged God's children to pray for all saints, and added, "Praying always with all prayer and supplication in the Spirit, and watching thereunto with all perseverance and supplication for all saints; And for me, that utterance may be given unto me, that I may open my mouth boldly, to make known the mystery of the gospel, For which I am an ambassador in bonds: that [in this] I may speak boldly, as I ought to speak" (Ephesians 6:18-20).

In his Epistle to the Colossians Paul made a similar request: "Continue in prayer, and watch in the same with thanksgiving . . . praying also for us, that God would open unto us a door of utterance, to speak the mystery of Christ, for which I am also in bonds" (Colossians 4:2-3).

Both of these verses spell out clearly that Paul was in prison because he preached the "mystery."

The two mysteries, the tares and the wheat, the false and the true, are seen in Christ's parable as existing together with similarity of appearance until the end of the age (Matthew 13:24-30,36-43). But there is a marked difference between the two. Both the false principle and the false person are exposed in the First Epistle of John. He informs us that the course of this age will be characterized by the presence of "many antichrists" (1 John 2:18). Now an antichrist is at once a person who both opposes Christ and who presents himself as Christ. The essential identifying mark of an antichrist is his renunciation of the mystery of godliness, or his denial of the essential deity and humanity of our Lord Jesus Christ. "Who is a [the] liar but he that denieth that Jesus is the Christ? He is antichrist, that denieth the Father and the Son" (1 John 2:22). "And every spirit that confesseth not that Jesus Christ is come in the flesh is not of God: and this is that spirit of antichrist, [of which] ye have heard that it should come; and even now already is it in the world" (1 John 4:3).

The antichrists were the progressive religious leaders in John's day who, like some religious leaders in our day, present the lie that Jesus was an exalted superman but that He was not God. Some ministers today tell us that it does not matter whether or not Christ is God. The identity of those who have the spirit of antichrist will show up when they are confronted with the crucial question, "What think ye of Christ?" To judge Jesus merely as a man is to accept the mystery of iniquity while denying the mystery of godliness. "For many deceivers are entered into the world, who confess not that Jesus Christ [cometh] in the flesh. This is a deceiver and an antichrist" (2 John 7).

The fundamental test of every person's faith is based upon his conception of Jesus Christ. Jesus is "Emmanuel, which being interpreted is, God with us" (Matthew 1:23). He is God "manifest in the flesh" (1 Timothy 3:16). This is the true Christian confession, and any denial of this truth is the spirit of antichrist. If these words strike the reader with a sense of horror; if they come to you with a sharp shock, then beware! Satan is the motivating force behind any and all denial that Jesus is God. The mystery of godliness is not a minor point for discussion or even debate; it represents everything upon which the whole Christian faith is built. The man Jesus, and God the eternal Son, are the same Person. He who denies this fact is none other than an antichrist. The "last hour" is an hour of strenuous conflict between the mystery of godliness and the mystery of iniquity.

THE MYSTERY OF INIQUITY

Our present world is heading toward the final stage of the conflict between the two seeds, the mystery of godliness and the mystery of iniquity. God is going to send Jesus Christ back to this earth, and in the meantime Satan is preparing his man, his masterpiece. The showdown will take place here on earth, culminating in the conflict of Armageddon. The seeds will have an eyeball-to-eyeball confrontation; the God-Man versus the Satan-man.

The term generally used to designate and describe this Satan-man is the Antichrist. Actually the word "antichrist" appears only five times, and all five references are in the Epistles of John (1 John 2:18,22; 4:3; 2 John 7). The word itself is never used of one particular person who is to come in the future, but rather of any and all persons who deny the mystery of godliness, the truth that God came to earth in the Person of Jesus Christ. All of Satan's "ministers" who appear "as the ministers of righteousness" are antichrists (2 Corinthians 11:15). Our Lord predicted that the end of the age would be characterized by "many false Christs" and "many false prophets" (Matthew 24:5,11,24). Is it possible that some of us who have been concentrating on the one Antichrist have failed to see clearly the function of the many antichrists?

However, when we examine other Scriptures, in both the Old and New Testaments, there seems to be one man to whom the antichrists will look for leadership. Many Bible teachers, some with minor disagreements, have identified the following with the Satan-man of the end time:

The "seed" of the serpent (Genesis 3:15).

The "little horn" (Daniel 7:7-8,20-26).

A "king of fierce countenance" (Daniel 8:23).

"The prince that shall come" (Daniel 9:26).

The king that "shall do according to his own will" (Daniel 11:16).

"That man of sin . . . the son of perdition" (2 Thessalonians 2:3).

"That Wicked [one]" (2 Thessalonians 2:8).

The "beast . . . out of the sea" (Revelation 13:1-10).

The point I would like to make is that, even though there will be more than one antichrist, Satan will have one man in control, his man, called "the son of perdition," Satan's chief son. When God planned His redemptive program, He

sent His Son. When Satan aims his final blow against God
and man, he will send his son. So the climactic conflict will
be the meeting of the two seeds, God's Seed who is Jesus
Christ, and Satan's seed who is an antichrist. John's prophecy
says that "the dragon [Satan] gave him his power, and his seat
[throne], and great authority" (Revelation 13:2). Where does
this man get his strength and authority? He gets it from Satan.
He will be Satan's superman, astute, aggressive, amiable,
academically alert, affable.

The activity of Satan and his demons is very real in the
earth now, but in that day man will witness and experience
the full manifestation of the mystery of iniquity. Many men
worship the devil today, but in that day "all that dwell upon
the earth shall worship him" (Revelation 13:4,8). Those who
refuse to worship him will do so under penalty of death
(Revelation 13:15).

WHEN WILL HE COME?

When will Satan's man appear and lead the masses
astray in matters of doctrine and behavior? When does this
leader of evil come on the scene? One passage that seems best
to answer this question is 2 Thessalonians 2. The Thessalonians
were troubled in their minds because of false teaching they
received. They were concerned lest they had already entered
the tribulation, called here "the day of the Lord" (verse 2
R.V.). Paul assured them that this was not the case and gives
two reasons why the tribulation had not yet arrived. The
first is that "a falling away" had not yet occurred; the second
is that "that man of sin" had not been made known on the
earth. The proof that they were not in the tribulation was
that the "seed" of the serpent, the "little horn" of Daniel 7,
the "king of fierce countenance" of Daniel 8, "the prince

that shall come" of Daniel 9, the king that "shall do according to his own will" of Daniel 11, the "beast . . . out of the sea" of Revelation 13, and described here by Paul, "that man of sin . . . the son of perdition . . . that Wicked [one]" (2 Thessalonians 2:3,8), had not yet come.

But how could they be sure that Satan's man was not then on the earth? For the same reason that we Christians today know that we are not now in the tribulation. There is a "restrainer" in the world holding back the full floodtide of evil. Paul said, "And now ye know what restraineth that he might be revealed in his time. For the mystery of iniquity doth already work: only he who now hindereth will continue to hinder until he be taken out of the way. And then shall that wicked one be revealed, whom the Lord shall consume with the spirit of His mouth, and shall destroy with the brightness of His coming" (2 Thessalonians 2:6-8).

The word "let" (verse 7) meant "hinder, or hold back, or restrain" at the time the King James Version of the Bible was prepared. This Old English use of the word has since changed, so that now "to let" means "to permit, to allow." Paul is simply saying that there is a power and a Person present in the world restraining Satan's man from putting in his appearance, and until that Person is removed, "that man of sin" cannot put in his appearance.

But who is this Restrainer? Anyone who has made a study of this question is acquainted with the many different answers that have been presented. Identifying the Restrainer is the debated issue in these verses. Commentators vary in their views from the Roman Empire, governments in general, to Satan himself.

The final decision as to the identity of the Restrainer cannot be made until the question is answered, Who is powerful enough to restrain Satan? Neither the Roman Empire nor human governments that followed were able to control lawlessness. Only God Himself can restrain Satan. We would not argue the point that God has used good government and good angels to restrain evil, but no one can deny that the power behind all enforced restraint must be God Himself.

The Holy Spirit in the Thessalonian passage is, in this writer's opinion, the Restrainer. The Holy Spirit in the world, dwelling in the Church corporately and in the Christian individually, is the One who restrains. Isaiah wrote, "When the enemy shall come in like a flood, the spirit of the LORD shall lift up a standard against him" (Isaiah 59:19). As long as Christ keeps His Church on earth Satan's man will not be appearing on the scene. That wicked one will be revealed in his true identity after the Church has been raptured.

Presently he is "the mystery of iniquity," veiled, covered from the view of all. But in his day the mystery will be unveiled, uncovered, revealed. Satan's plan calls for an all-out demonstration of lawlessness without restraint, when men and women, under his control, will give themselves to most vile thoughts, words, and actions. The lawlessness and vice we are witnessing in the world today is tame compared with coming world conditions when Satan's man rules.

DARK DAYS ARE AHEAD!

A most somber period lies ahead for the people on this earth. None of us enjoy discussing a future that looks foreboding. But why shouldn't we face the facts? The Bible has been accurate in its predictions to date, therefore we would be foolish to play the ostrich role now. Ignoring the facts can do us no good. Jesus said, "The truth shall make you free" (John 8:32).

Let's face it! We are bankrupt morally, economically, and politically. But the worst is yet to be. The appearing of "*that* man of sin" will introduce a period of misery and hardship unprecedented in human history. Since world conditions are as bad as they are with the restraining power of the Holy Spirit and the Church in the world, we need not stretch the imagination to guess what the situation will be after the Spirit and the Church are gone and "*that* wicked one" takes over. Our Lord's description of those days tells the true story: "For then shall be great tribulation, such as was not since the beginning of the world to this time, no, nor ever shall be" (Matthew 24:21).

Jeremiah described that period as follows: "Alas! for that day is great, so that none is like it: it is even the time of Jacob's trouble; but he shall be saved out of it" (Jeremiah 30:7).

Daniel predicted that time in vivid terms: "And there shall be a time of trouble, such as never was since there was

71

a nation even to that time" (Daniel 12:1).

Joel, inspired by the Holy Spirit, as was Jeremiah and Daniel, wrote, "A day of darkness and of gloominess, a day of clouds and of thick darkness, as the morning spread upon the mountains: a great people and a strong; there hath not been ever the like, neither shall be any more after it, even to the years of many generations" (Joel 2:2).

Now have a close look at those descriptive statements from Jesus, Jeremiah, Daniel, and Joel. Inasmuch as only one time can be worse than another, it is obvious that all four are referring to the same period "Great tribulation . . . trouble . . . gloominess"—these are terms depicting unpleasant conditions, to say the least. To a certain degree we are witnessing events now which indicate the setting of the stage for those coming judgments. But during the Great Tribulation they reach an unprecedented degree of severity.

One day in the future, how soon we do not know, a startling phenomenon will occur. The earth's population will be made aware of the fact that a large number of their fellow men will have mysteriously disappeared. From every walk of life, government, the business office, the factory, the classroom, the home, there will be many vacancies as the result of those who are caught up to meet the Lord in the air. This event will not be local but earth-wide. Frankly, I have a feeling that many who will be left on the earth will be aware of what has taken place. The appearing of Christ to rapture the Church is already a widely heralded event. Unbelievers may sneer and scoff at the idea of Christ's coming to gather His people and take them to Heaven, but at least they have heard it.

It is to the state of affairs on earth, after the true Church of Christ is taken away, that we will now give attention. We are not left to guessing or to using our imagination. The Word of God has much to say on the subject.

THE DURATION OF THE PERIOD

The first clue as to the duration of that time of trouble comes from Daniel's vision of the seventy weeks (Daniel 9:24-27). The Hebrew word translated "weeks" means "seven," just as our English word "dozen" means "twelve." The weeks in Daniel's vision are not weeks of days, but weeks of years, an idea with which the Jews were quite familiar. The seventy weeks (seven) of years (70 times 7 or 490 years) comprise a time period during which certain events would occur.

The 490 years (70 weeks) were divided into three periods, a group of seven, a group of sixty-two, and one. The first two periods, seven and sixty-two, a total of sixty-nine weeks (483 years), would culminate in the coming and crucifixion of Christ the Messiah, and the destruction of "the city and the sanctuary" (Daniel 9:25-26). The reference to "the city and the sanctuary" is to the destruction of Jerusalem and the temple in A.D. 70, approximately forty years after our Lord's crucifixion. The prophecies relating to the sixty-nine weeks (483 years) have been fulfilled, so for us today this is now history.

But it is the third division of the total period, the seventieth week (seven years), which is still future awaiting fulfillment. This is that time of "tribulation, trouble, and gloominess." We will not here discuss the evidences for the time gap between the sixty-ninth and seventieth weeks, only to point out the fact that Daniel's description of events during the seventieth week (seven years) fits perfectly the description of the tribulation in other passages, particularly our Lord's description given in His Olivet discourse (Matthew 24:15). The period under discussion, then, will last seven years and will follow the removal of Christ's Church from the earth.

THE DIVISION OF THE PERIOD

The tribulation week is of seven years duration, but it is to be noted that this period is divided into two equal halves of three-and-a-half years each.

Daniel speaks of a significant event to occur "in the midst of the week" (Daniel 9:27), or at the end of the first three-and-a-half years. This twofold division of the seven years is designated in several places in Scripture and by different terms: "A time [1], and times [2], and half a time [½]" (Revelation 12:14). The one, two, and one-half equal three-and-one-half. "A thousand two hundred and threescore days" (Revelation 12:6). "Forty and two months" (Revelation 11:2; 13:5).

These terms all have reference to one-half of Daniel's seventieth week. In two of his visions that period is described as "a time [1] and times [2] and the dividing of time [½]" (Daniel 7:25), and "a time, times, and an half" (Daniel 12:7).

THE DESOLATION OF THE PERIOD

Upon whom are the judgments of those coming dark days determined? To this question the Bible gives two clear answers: It is "the time of Jacob's trouble" (Jeremiah 30:7). "It shall be the time of the heathen" [Gentiles] (Ezekiel 30:3). Both Israel and the Gentile nations are included in the purpose of the coming judgments upon the earth. All men are sinners, and all who have rejected God's Son must come to a time of reckoning, a time of retribution.

First, Israel must go through the furnace of affliction for her final purification and preparation to receive Jesus Christ as her Messiah. Israel's return to the Land resulted in the fulfillment of many prophecies. The desert is flourishing as a rose (Isaiah 32:13,15; 35:1-2; 41:19). The ruins have been rebuilt and the population has increased (Isaiah 61:4; Jeremiah 33:10-11; Ezekiel 36:10-11; 33-38). Economically the nation has continued to prosper (Isaiah 60:5,9,17). Technologically there have been great strides made. But with all of these prophecies fulfilled, the grievous fact remains that Jesus Christ is still rejected as Israel's Messiah.

One of the first moves that Satan's man will make is to seduce Israel into an alliance. He will present himself to Israel as her messiah for whom she will be waiting. The covenant will be made for seven years (Daniel 9:27). The reasonableness of such a treaty is understandable. Israel does not have many friends now, nor will her friends increase in the future. It is not difficult to see how Israel will respond to the overtures of such an astute person as the man of sin. As long as Satan's man continues to fulfill the agreement in the treaty, Israel will have reason to feel secure. A feeling of security for the Jews will be a pleasant change from their past. The stress and tension from Arab pressures will be greatly reduced during the first three-and-a-half years of tribulation. The people of the Land will have reason to believe that their fortunes have changed for the better.

But midway in that seven-year period the entire situation will change. Satan's man will break the covenant he made with Israel. Daniel predicted that desolations are determined upon the city and the sanctuary (9:27). In the middle of the week the "abomination of desolation" will come and wrath will be poured out upon the people, the city, and the temple (Matthew 24:15). Since the subject of Daniel's prophecy is the Jews, "Thy people" (9:24), those final three-and-one-half years will be a time of intense suffering for Israel.

What prompts the devil-man to act as he does? At that time the temple will be rebuilt and functioning as the place of worship, "the holy place" (Matthew 24:15). But the enemy of God and His people will not tolerate the function again of the ancient Levitical priesthood and offerings. What Satan permitted to be started he will end abruptly. He will not allow any religious rivalry.

His ultimate sin will not be merely his refusal to allow the Jews to worship Jehovah, but the fact that he exalts himself "above all that is called God, or that is worshipped; so that he as God sitteth in the temple of God, shewing himself that he is God" (2 Thessalonians 2:4). At last the devil will succeed in having himself worshiped by all the people in the earth, except those persons who are saved after the rapture of the Church (Revelation 13:4, 8,15). This has been his goal since the day he deceived our first parents.

This man of sin, who is the incarnation of Satan, actually declares himself to be the incarnation of God. Here the "opposer" is definitely linked with Satan the "adversary" in 1 Timothy 5:14, where the same participle is used. The religious system of the man of sin will claim first place over the one true God and all false gods. This is the abomination of desolation. This mysterious person, who in all probability will be a Jew, is described by Daniel as "the king [that] shall do according to his will; and he shall exalt himself, and magnify himself above every god, and shall speak marvellous things against the God of gods, and shall prosper till the indignation be accomplished: for that that is determined shall be done. Neither shall he regard the God of his fathers, nor the desire of women, nor regard any god: for he shall magnify himself above all" (Daniel 11:36-37). This daring action of the man of sin leads to his complete takeover of the temple of God and the whole system of worship. It is the fulfillment of our Lord's prediction, "I am come in My Father's name, and ye receive Me not: if another ... come in his own name, him ye will receive" (John 5:43). This is Satan's final and futile attempt to dethrone God, the abomination of desolation.

THE DECEPTION OF THE PERIOD

In studying the history of Satan we have seen that deception has always been his specialty. Paul wrote that "the serpent *beguiled* Eve" (2 Corinthians 11:3), and "the woman being *deceived* was in the transgression" (1 Timothy 2:14). After the Church has been raptured John saw "that old serpent, called the Devil, and Satan, which *deceiveth* the whole world" (Revelation 12:9). The reason he will be incarcerated during Christ's reign on earth is "that he should *deceive* the nations no more, till the thousand years should be fulfilled. . . . And when the thousand years are expired, Satan shall be loosed out of his prison. And shall go out to *deceive* the nations" (Revelation 20:3,7-8). His demons also are called "seducing [deceiving] spirits" (1 Timothy 4:1). Most assuredly deceit is one of the "wiles of the devil" (Ephesians 6:11). It is one of the "devices" by which he seeks to "get an advantage of us" (2 Corinthians 2:11).

Since the mystery of iniquity is Satan's masterpiece, one can imagine the widespread deception after the Church has been taken from the earth. The Church is God's great masterpiece, restraining the mystery of iniquity and Satan's artful deception, thus the Church is the devil's great antagonist. As the age draws to a close, we may expect satanic deception to increase, and then, after the rapture of the Church, it will reach an all-time high. Jesus gave a brief description of demonic deception in the "great tribulation." He said, "For there shall arise false Christs, and false prophets, and shall shew great signs and wonders; insomuch that, if it were possible, they shall deceive the very elect" (Matthew 24:24).

Paul gave us a passage which is a close parallel to our Lord's. The apostle describes the "last days" (2 Timothy 3:1), an expression which refers to the consummation of the age immediately preceding the Second Advent of the Lord Jesus Christ. Those "times" he describes as "perilous," meaning *grievous* and *difficult*, a time when evil would combine its forces for its final assault. The word translated perilous is *chalepos*, the same word used in Matthew 8:28 to describe the two demon-possessed men who met Jesus among the tombs. Those men were violent and dangerous maniacs. They were a threat to society.

Here Paul presents a picture of the final showdown with satanic forces. In the context he lists several characteristics of the end times, all of which constitute the terrible and ghastly qualities of godlessness. He describes mankind as "Having a form of godliness, but denying the power thereof" (2 Timothy 3:5). There will be religion without reality, without life. Someone described it as "unchristian Christianity." It is all mere formality.

In our apartment in Florida we had a beautifully designed chair that we wouldn't dare sit on. Small white termites had eaten away the inside of the frame, leaving us with the outward shell. The profession in the "last days" will be but an empty shell, an outer veneer.

Now you might be wondering how so many people could be so horribly deceived. It is Satan's strategy to deceive by imitation, by counterfeit. The Apostle John calls it "the depths of Satan" (Revelation 2:24). Satan will have his connoisseurs of counterfeit going from house to house. Their activity is largely directed toward women who are restless, unhappy, and fearful. Allow the inspired witness to describe that situation: "For of this sort are they which creep into houses, and lead captive silly women laden with sins, led away with divers lusts, Ever learning, and never able to come to the knowledge of the truth" (2 Timothy 3:6-7). Many men are just as weak and unstable, but history shows that the "creeps" prey on women, a pattern set by Satan when he first seduced Eve. Kenneth S. Wuest said, "One of the great virtues of womanhood, namely, that of trusting another, is turned into a weakness by Satan here" (*The Pastoral Epistles*, page 146). It has always been so that exponents of all religions find their easiest victims among a certain class of gullible women who enjoy secret instruction and occult solutions to problems. They are willing to learn from anyone, yet never able to come to a knowledge of the truth.

This clever deception by imitation is now illustrated by two men, Jannes and Jambres (2 Timothy 3:8). Those men are not named in the Old Testament itself, but some scholars are agreed that they are the two court magicians of Pharaoh who imitated the miracles of Moses and Aaron in Exodus 7:11; 8:7; and 9:11. They stand out as Satan's representative men who seek to frustrate the purposes of God by deceptive imitation.

When the devil's sinister man appears, it will be "after the working of Satan with all power and signs and lying wonders, And with all *deceivableness* of unrighteousness in them that perish; because they received not the love of the truth, that they might be saved" (2 Thessalonians 2:9-10). The man of sin will oppose the truth by means of his deceptive counterfeit. The future after the rapture is not bright, but black!

A thorough brain-washing is in store for earth's population. Satan's antichrists, under the supervision of the man of sin, will control the news media totally. The presentation of news events will be tailored so as to control the minds of everyone. By seduction and ruse Satan will have all of humanity at his feet.

THE DEVASTATION OF THE PERIOD

The Old Testament prophets had much to say about the judgments of the end time. The term they used most frequently to describe that devastating period is called the day of the Lord. It is not a twenty-four hour day, but a period of time when God vindicates His holiness in His judgment against sin.

Isaiah. "For the *day of the LORD* of hosts shall be upon every one that is proud and lofty, and upon every one that is lifted up; and he shall be brought low. . . . Howl ye; for the *day of the LORD* is at hand; it shall come as a *destruction* from the Almighty. . . . Behold, the *day of the LORD* cometh, cruel both with wrath and fierce anger, to lay the land *desolate*: and He shall *destroy* the sinners thereof out of it. . . . And I will punish the world for their evil, and the wicked for their iniquity" (Isaiah 2:12; 13:6,9,11).

Jeremiah. "For this is the *day of the Lord* GOD of hosts, a day of vengeance, that He may avenge Him of His adversaries: and the sword shall devour" (Jeremiah 46:10).

Ezekiel. "For the day is near, even the *day of the LORD* is near, a cloudy day; it shall be the time of the heathen [Gentiles] " (Ezekiel 30:3).

Joel. "Alas for the day! for the *day of the LORD* is at hand, and as a *destruction* from the Almighty shall it come. . . . Blow ye the trumpet in Zion, and sound an alarm in My holy mountain: let all the inhabitants of the land tremble: for the *day of the LORD* cometh, for it is nigh at hand; A day of *darkness* and of gloominess . . . for the *day of the LORD* is great and very terrible; and who can abide it? . . . The sun shall be turned into *darkness*, and the moon into blood, before the great and the terrible *day of the LORD* come" (Joel 1:15; 2:1-2,11,31).

Amos. "Woe unto you that desire the *day of the LORD!* to what end is it for you? The *day of the LORD* is *darkness*, and not light. . . . Shall not the *day of the LORD* be *darkness*, and not light? Even very *dark*, and no brightness in it?" (Amos 5:18,20)

Obadiah. "For the *day of the LORD* is near upon all the heathen [Gentiles]: as thou hast done, it shall be done unto thee: thy reward shall return upon thine own head" (Obadiah 15).

Zephaniah. "The great *day of the LORD* is near, it is near, and hasteth greatly, even the voice of the *day of the LORD*: the mighty man shall cry there bitterly. That day is a day of wrath, a day of trouble and *distress*, a day of wasteness and *desolation*, a day of *darkness* and gloominess, a day of clouds and thick *darkness*. . . . And I will bring distress upon men, that they shall walk like blind men, because they have sinned against the LORD: and their blood shall be poured out as dust, and their flesh as the dung. Neither their silver nor their gold shall be able to deliver them in the day of the *LORD'S* wrath; but the whole land shall be *devoured* by the fire of His jealousy: for He shall make even a speedy riddance of all them that dwell in the land" (Zephaniah 1:14-15,17-18).

The italics in the above verses are mine. I am impressed with the prophets' description of the *day of the LORD: destruction, desolation, darkness, distress, devoured.* These terms describe the punishments deserved because of sin. When evil will have reached its greatest climax, then judgment attains its highest degree of severity. The holiness of God demands that sin be punished. When that man of sin, Satan's man, controls the world, then God will deal with men in His wrath (Psalm 2:5), using that wicked one to accomplish His purpose. The Psalmist wrote, "Surely the wrath of man shall praise Thee" (Psalm 76:10). Anyone reading these fearful passages from God's Word can see beyond doubt that the world is moving toward tragic times.

Now add to these Old Testament predictions the prophecies in the New Testament which speak of coming judgment, and you will see that the frightful retribution awaiting the world exceeds the powers of description.

There will be unprecedented war engulfing the entire world (compare Matthew 24:6-7 with Revelation 6:3-4); unexampled famine which is the necessary complement of war (Amos 8:11-12; compare Matthew 24:7 with Revelation 6:5-6); unparalleled natural calamities such as earthquakes (Luke 21:11; Revelation 6:12-14; 8:5; 11:13,19; 16:17-20); unmatched religious persecution (Matthew 24:8-10; Luke 21:12-19; 2 Thessalonians 2:3-4; Revelation 6:9-11); unlimited scourges on the vegetation of the earth (Revelation 8:7; 9:3). All of this devastation, destruction, darkness, and distress will cause an unusual number of people to seek death (Revelation 9:6). "For then shall be great tribulation, such as was not since the beginning of the world to this time, no, nor ever shall be" (Matthew 24:21).

Today many turn a deaf ear to the gospel. They avoid the churches where God's Word is declared, and treat lightly the prediction of coming judgment. But all those warnings are a display of God's grace calling upon people everywhere to repent and receive Jesus Christ.

THE DELIVERANCE OF THE PERIOD

In Joel's prophecy of the coming "day of the LORD," there is a bright note. "And it shall come to pass, that whosoever shall call on the name of the LORD shall be delivered: for in mount Zion and . . . Jerusalem shall be deliverance, as the LORD hath said, and in the remnant whom the LORD shall call" (Joel 2:32).

The Lord Jesus sounded the same note when He said, "And this gospel of the kingdom shall be preached in all the world for a witness unto all nations; and then shall the end come" (Matthew 24:14).

Here is an encouraging sign of the last days. In the midst of divine retribution there is redemption. Many who have never heard the gospel will have their chance to be saved. Among those converted will be a substantial number of Jews. During the tribulation a sizable group of Jews will go forth preaching the gospel of the kingdom (Revelation 7:1-8). The 144,000 will be sealed as "the servants of our God" for protection against the devastation of those days. When the judgment of the fifth trumpet is introduced, specific instruction is given to inflict "only those men which have not the seal of God in their foreheads" (Revelation 9:4). This greater degree of protection for the 144,000 is God's special care of His servants against Satan's sinister man and the punishment to be meted out to unbelievers.

Every tribe of Israel will be represented in that band of gospel preachers, 12,000 from each tribe. Toward the end of the tribulation the same group is mentioned again, with Christ standing with them and "His Father's name written in their foreheads." They are singing the song of redemption having been "redeemed from among men" (Revelation 14:1-5). Many expositors see in Revelation 7:9 an innumerable host of converts resulting from the preaching of the 144,000. Just as "Noah found grace in the eyes of the LORD" in the judgment of the flood (Genesis 6:8), even so will many be saved during the tribulation.

An additional "two witnesses" will be raised up by God to preach to many during the last half of the tribulation

(Revelation 11:3-13). They will commence their witnessing about the time Satan's man of sin breaks his agreement with Israel. They will receive the much needed empowering of the Holy Spirit for their daring task of witnessing and working miracles. At the conclusion of their ministry, a mighty earthquake destroys one-tenth of the city, killing no less than 2,000 people. But in the midst of human misery there is divine mercy. During all seven years of Daniel's seventieth week God will have His faithful witnesses disseminating His good news of salvation.

God does not content Himself with judgment. He must judge sin because His holiness demands it. He "will have all men to be saved, and to come unto the knowledge of the truth" (1 Timothy 2:4). God "is longsuffering to us-ward, not willing that any should perish, but that all should come to repentance" (2 Peter 3:9). If we are correct in our interpretation of Zechariah 13:8, a third of the people on the earth will be saved during the tribulation. Many will be martyred for their acceptance of Jesus Christ and their refusal to worship Satan, but they will be in Heaven (Revelation 7:9,14-15; 13:8,15). In the midst of the final judgments to come upon the earth, God in His grace will not allow one believing heart to be cast into the lake of fire.

But every unsaved person should be warned. If you have rejected the Lord Jesus Christ as your Saviour at the time of the rapture, you will not be saved during the tribulation. If you suppress the truth now, God will permit Satan's man of sin to delude you (2 Thessalonians 2:9-12). Those persons who will be saved during the tribulation will come, for the most part, from those parts of the world not yet reached with the gospel. Your only escape is to believe now on the Lord Jesus Christ, and be saved (Acts 16:31).

THANK GOD FOR GOOD ANGELS

Angels are for real! To deny the existence of angels is to deny the authority of the Scriptures. The fact that they are mentioned not less than two hundred and sixty times in the Bible is indisputable evidence that they are specific beings.

Even liberal theologians and some scientists, who at one time attributed the idea of angels and demons to superstition, are now acknowledging the possibility of the existence of invisible intelligent beings. This new interest has taken on a dangerous dimension, exciting an exploratory curiosity on the part of many people. Unfortunately the investigations for the most part are in the pursuit of evil spirits and their activity.

But God has His good angels, His holy ones in the spirit world. These too, as do the demons, function on planet earth and affect the activities of man. The good angels have been active throughout all of human history, and their intervention in the affairs of man is no less active today. As we approach the "last days" with increased activity on the part of demons, we may be certain that there will be a corresponding activity on the part of God's good angels.

THE ORIGIN OF ANGELS

In the Biblical account of creation there is no specific mention of angels. The heavens are mentioned in the creation story (Genesis 1:1), but there is no specific, or even casual, discussion of the creation of those spirit beings who inhabit the heavens. The fact of the creation of angels by God is suggested in Paul's Epistle to the Colossians. The apostle wrote, "For by Him were all things created, that are in heaven, and that are in earth, visible and invisible, whether they be thrones, or dominions, or principalities, or powers: all things were created by Him, and for Him" (Colossians 1:16).

Of course the word "angel" does not appear in this passage, but it does seem evident that Paul includes them under the titles of "thrones, dominions, principalities, and powers." These are terms Paul used elsewhere when referring to these spirit beings as a part of "all things created, that are in heaven . . . invisible" (see Romans 8:38; Ephesians 3:10; Colossians 2:15).

It was by Christ and for Christ that all things were created (John 1:3), and "by Him all things consist" (Colossians 1:17), meaning that by Him all things cohere, or hold together. He is the cause of creation and the consummation of creation, and between the cause and the consummation, during the present time as we know it, Christ is still in charge of things. He may allow wicked spirits to punish or chasten men for their sins, but they cannot act without His permissive will. Even so the good angels carry out His every wish. He said to Peter, "Thinkest thou that I cannot now pray to My Father, and He shall presently give Me more than twelve legions of angels?" (Matthew 26:53)

In the Colossian passage Christ is seen as "the first-born of every creature" ("creation" in the R.V. Colossians 1:15). Do not twist this statement and thereby attach to it a wrong meaning. It does not mean that Christ is a created being, or the first person to be created. The word "first-born" (Greek, *prototokos*) is not limited to a time significance. William Barclay points out the fact that "firstborn" is very commonly a title of *honor*. Israel, for instance, as a nation is the firstborn son of God (Exodus 4:22). The meaning of that phrase is that the nation of Israel is the chosen, the most honored, and the most favored.

Secondly, we must note that "Firstborn" is a title of the Messiah, as the Jews themselves interpreted it (Psalm 89:27). Clearly the word "firstborn" is not used in a time sense at all, but in the sense of special honor. (William Barclay, *(The Letters to the Philippians, Colossians, and Thessalonians,* page 143.) Before all creation Christ was honored above all that He would create. Thus His rule extends over all the cosmic forces and created beings of the universe, including angels. "Being made so much better than the angels, as He hath by inheritance obtained a more excellent name than they" (Hebrews 1:4).

Christ is the honored Son while angels are His created beings who serve Him. Angels are never to be worshiped, rather they are Christ's subjects who worship Him. The divine command is spelled out clearly, "And let all the angels of God worship Him" (Hebrews 1:6). "Let no man beguile you of your reward in . . . worshipping of angels" (Colossians 2:18).

Peter stressed the fact that Christ is now in Heaven on the right hand of God, "Angels and authorities and powers being made subject unto Him" (1 Peter 3:22). It is good news for Christians to know that a part of Christ's present ministry in their behalf is to send His angels to assist them. "Are they not all ministering spirits, sent forth to minister for them who shall be heirs of salvation?" (Hebrews 1:14)

WHEN WERE THE ANGELS CREATED?

The time of their creation is not stated definitely in Scripture. However, there is at least one passage which infers that angels were created before man, in the beginning when God created the heavens and the earth. We know that Satan is a fallen angel, and it appears evident that he had been created and had fallen before the creation of Adam and Eve.

Dr. Francis Peiper said, "They were created within the hexaemeron (the six days of creation in Genesis). They were not created before the universe, because before the universe there was only God (John 1:1-3). They were not created after the universe, because after the creation of the universe God rested from all His work (Genesis 2:2-3). On which day of the hexaemeron they were created cannot be determined with certainty, because Scripture is silent on this point" (Francis Peiper, *Christian Dogmatics,* Volume I, page 499).

Some teachers hold that angels were created at the time the universe was created. Charles F. Baker says: "Those who hold the gap theory of Genesis 1:2, and who also associate the fall of Satan and his angels with the chaos of that verse, would have to make the creation of angels a part of the original creation. Any view, however, to square with the facts, would have to make the creation of angels antedate that of man" (Charles F. Baker, *A Dispensational Theology*, page 216).

It seems to this writer that angels might have been created before the physical universe and man. God asked Job, "Where wast thou when I laid the foundations of the earth. . . . When the morning stars sang together, and all the sons of God shouted for joy?" (Job 38:4,7)

I take it that "the sons of God" here are angels, the same as in Job 1:6 and 2:1. If this view is correct, then the angels were created first. However, we suggest caution against dogmatism in this area.

THE NUMBER OF ANGELS

The Epistle to the Hebrews has a comment on the number of angels: "But ye are come unto mount Sion, and unto the city of the living God, the heavenly Jerusalem, and to an innumerable company of angels" (Hebrews 12:22).

This verse tells us that there is a great host of angels. When Moses related the giving of the Law at Sinai, he said, "The LORD came . . . with ten thousands of saints" (Deuteronomy 33:2). Daniel saw in one of his visions "thousand thousands ministering unto Him, and ten thousand times ten thousand stood before Him" (Daniel 7:10). The Psalmist wrote, "The chariots of God are twenty thousand, even thousands of angels" (Psalm 68:17). When John saw the Lamb take the scroll, he said, "And I beheld, and I heard the voice of many angels round about the throne and the beasts and the elders: and the number of them was ten thousand times ten thousand, and thousands of thousands" (Revelation 5:11). We may find courage and comfort in the fact that so great a company of holy angels stand ready at all times to minister in behalf of God's children.

In 2 Kings 6, the king of Syria had planned by wicked stealth to destroy Israel. The Prophet Elisha, knowing of the evil plot, warned Israel's king so that the nation was spared. Then Elisha and his servant slipped away to Dothan for a time of quiet communion with God.

The king of Syria, angry with Elisha because he spoiled his well-laid plans, heard that Elisha was in Dothan. The king sent a large unit of his army to encircle the city and capture Elisha. Early in the morning Elisha's servant detected the huge army surrounding Dothan. He hurried to the prophet of God and said, "Alas, my master! how shall we do?"

"And he answered, Fear not: for they that be with us are more than they that be with them. And Elisha prayed, and said, LORD, I pray Thee, open his eyes, that he may see. And the LORD opened the eyes of the young man; and he saw: and, behold, the mountain was full of horses and chariots of fire round about Elisha. And when they came down to him, Elisha prayed unto the LORD, and said, Smite this people, I pray Thee, with blindness. And He smote them with blindness according to the word of Elisha" (2 Kings 6:16-18).

In this most dramatic scene we have an amazing event. God had his host of angels to surround His child and smite the entire Syrian army with blindness. How many soldiers there were in the Syrian army we are not told, but Elisha knew that "they that be with us are more than they that be with them."

We may feel very much outnumbered by the evil forces that surround, but God has His angels that are for us, and they are greater than those that are against us. If we walk in the will of God we are immortal until God has finished His work in and through us. Thank God for His good angels.

THE ORDER OF ANGELS

In the Old Testament one of the titles of Jehovah is *Lord of Hosts* (Jehovah Sabaoth), appearing more times in Scripture than any other of God's names. The word *sabaoth* means "to bring together, to assemble," usually the idea being to assemble for warfare. This is God's military name, and the *hosts* are His armies that He assembles for the protection of His people. (In some passages the "hosts of heaven" may refer to the stars, as in Genesis 2:1-2; Deuteronomy 4:19.)

Now an innumerable host of angels assembled for action would need to be organized. Since "God is not the author of confusion" (1 Corinthians 14:33), we may assume that His angel forces would be well arranged in orderly fashion. There are different classifications of angels, different ranks and grades.

The Cherubim. The words "cherub" and "cherubim" are mentioned not less than eighty-five times in the Bible, all of them appearing in the Old Testament except one in Hebrews 9:5. These are angels, great in might and intelligence. Cherubim were stationed at the entrance to the garden of Eden after man was expelled (Genesis 3:24). The clearest description of them is found in Ezekiel 1:10; 9:3; 10:15-22. Two gold cherub figures adorned the ark (Exodus 25:17-22), and two replicas adorned Solomon's temple (1 Kings 6:23-28). An examination of these Scriptures indicate that the cherubim were called to the special ministry of guarding the holiness of God. Their appearance in the tabernacle and temple was an aid to the worshiper, reminding him that God is holy and therefore cannot condone sin. This lesson would be drawn from their first mention in Scripture (Genesis 3:24). We see them in the last book in the Bible where, as "beasts" (Greek, *zoon,* translated "living creatures" in the R.V.) "they rest not day and night, saying, Holy, holy, holy, Lord God Almighty, which was, and is, and is to come" (Revelation 4:6-9).

The Seraphim. There appears to be only one mention of them in Scripture, in connection with Isaiah's vision of the Lord in Isaiah 6:1-6. Like the cherubim, they too are concerned with the holiness of God. But more specifically their ministry is related to the cleansing of the sinner. Their ministry in the Isaiah passage was to cleanse Isaiah's uncleanliness by touching his life with a live coal from off the altar.

The Archangel. The Bible speaks of only one archangel,

named Michael. His name means, "who is like God." It is questionable to speak of "archangels" in the plural. His special ministry in Old Testament times was in defense of Israel (Daniel 10:13,21). He is called "one of the chief princes . . . which standeth for the children of thy people" (Daniel 10:13; 12:1). He was not a communicating angel with a prophetic message, as was Gabriel, but the angel-prince of mighty power endued with military skill to defend Israel against her enemies, seen and unseen.

There is a reference to the archangel in 1 Thessalonians 4:16: "For the Lord Himself shall descend from heaven with a shout, with the voice of the archangel, and with the trump of God: and the dead in Christ shall rise first" (1 Thessalonians 4:16). This verse raises some questions which are not answered easily. In the Greek there is not the definite article. It is *an* archangel, not *the* archangel. This has led some commentators to conclude that there are other archangels. At any rate, God will have one of His military leaders present at the rapture, possibly to prevent any hindrance through satanic intervention. Thank God for His good angels.

GABRIEL—GOD'S SPECIAL DELIVERY MESSENGER

One of the special angels named in the Bible is *Gabriel.* His ministry was chiefly that of dispatching messages directly from God to persons on earth. Before God revealed Himself and His plans in His written Word, the Bible, He would commission angels from time to time to deliver vital information. Twice in the book of Daniel we see Gabriel delivering special communiques (Daniel 8:15-27; 9:20-27). The latter appearance to Daniel brought from God one of the most amazing prophecies in the Old Testament.

After Gabriel delivered his two messages to Daniel, he

is not mentioned again in the Bible until he appeared to the aged priest Zacharias. When Gabriel came to Zacharias he was in the temple praying about a very personal matter. He and his wife Elisabeth had no children of their own, and so Zacharias unburdened his heart to the Lord. While he was in prayer, Gabriel appeared on the right side of the altar of incense, and said to him, "Fear not, Zacharias: for thy prayer is heard; and thy wife Elisabeth shall bear thee a son, and thou shalt call his name John" (Luke 1:5-20). Now that was a most significant announcement because it heralded the coming of the forerunner of our Lord Jesus Christ. God was about to set aside the laws of nature and perform a miracle. The announcement was so unusual that God dispatched His heavenly messenger to deliver the good word to Zacharias personally.

Having fulfilled his mission faithfully, Gabriel returned to Heaven to await his next assignment. It came approximately six months later when God sent him to earth again, this time to a woman. This was doubtless Gabriel's most important assignment for he was now about to dispatch to planet earth the greatest news that ever came from Heaven. The content of his message was a startling revelation to its recipient, the Virgin Mary. Gabriel well-nigh shocked her with God's announcement that she would soon become pregnant and her child would be the long expected Messiah (Luke 1:26-37). Subjecting her will to the will of God, Mary yielded her total person—body, soul, and spirit. I have often wondered how God's good angels might feel when they listen to men deny the Virgin Birth of our Lord Jesus Christ.

Gabriel returned to Heaven, having completed his assignment faithfully, and there is no further mention of him in Scripture. What his activity has been since then, we might never know. We dare not go beyond what is written in God's Word, and it is unwise to speculate. We do know that angels never die (Luke 20:36), so there is that possibility of meeting Gabriel some day. If we do have the experience of greeting this good angel, it will be a great privilege to come face to face with one of God's messengers who carried out every assignment faithfully. I have an idea that, even in that day, we will thank God for His good angels.

THE MINISTRY OF ANGELS

God's good angels have a special interest in children. Jesus said, "Take heed that ye despise not one of these little ones; for I say unto you, That in heaven their angels do always behold the face of My Father which is in heaven" (Matthew 18:10). What did Jesus mean by "their angels"? It could be that God has appointed certain angels to the specialized ministry of protecting little children against evil forces. "The angel of the LORD encampeth round about them that fear Him, and delivereth them" (Psalm 34:7). I believe our Lord intended to give encouragement concerning little ones, but at the same time He warns adults against neglecting them. Children mean much to the Lord, and He will provide His glorious creatures to safeguard them. Let us never impose upon the Lord and His good angels, but rather heed His final instruction, "Despise not one of these little ones."

Angels demonstrated miraculous power on behalf of Christ's servants. Read the exciting and amusing story of the apostles' deliverance from prison in Acts 5:17-23. The Sadducees were so envious of the apostles, they had them committed to prison. "But the angel of the Lord by night opened the prison doors, and brought them forth" (Acts 5:19). On a former occasion they were delivered from prison by their enemies (Acts 4:21), but here they are delivered by the miraculous power of a messenger sent from Heaven, "the angel of the Lord." Picking prison locks is no problem for one of God's good angels. The enemies of Christ know how to put His servants into jail, but His angels know how to get them out.

The events recorded by Luke in the book of Acts surround the greatest movement of God in human history. It was an angel of the Lord who guided Philip (Acts 8:26), and Cornelius (Acts 10:3,30-32). An angel delivered Peter from two iron chains that bound him, and together the angel and Peter walked past the guards unnoticed (Acts 12:5-9). An angel encouraged and strengthened Paul on a perilous sea voyage (Acts 27:14-25). Thank God for His good angels.

Corrie ten Boom relates an incident as follows:

One day, on a trip to Russia, I approached the customs officer with a suitcase full of Russian Bibles. I stood in the line and saw how carefully the customs officers checked every suitcase. Suddenly a great fear swept over me. "What will he do when he finds my Bibles? Send me back to Holland? Put me in prison?"

I closed my eyes to shut out the scene around me and said, "Lord, in Jeremiah 1, it is written that God watches over His Word to perform it [verse 12]. Lord, the Bibles in my suitcase are Your Word. Now, God, please watch over Your Word—my Bibles—so I may take them to Your people in Russia."

Now I know that is not what Jeremiah meant, but I have found that if I pray with my hand on the promises of the open Bible I do not have to wait until my position is doctrinally sound. God sees my heart.

The moment I prayed I opened my eyes and saw around my suitcase light beings. They were angels. It was the first and only time in my life that I had ever seen them, although I had known many, many times they were present. But this time I saw them, only for a moment, and then they were gone. But so was my fear.

I moved on through the customs line, sliding my suitcase along the stainless steel table toward the officer who was doing such a thorough inspection. At last I was before him.

"Is this your suitcase?" he asked.

"Yes, sir," I answered politely.

"It seems very heavy," he said, grasping it by the handle and picking it up.

"It is very heavy," I said.

He smiled. "Since you are the last one to come through the line I now have time to help you. If you will follow me I shall carry it for you out to your taxi." (*Tramp for the Lord,* by Corrie ten Boom with Jamie Buckingham, Fleming H. Revell Company, pages 188-189)

Are we to be surprised that God sent angels to minister to Corrie ten Boom? The first mention in the Bible of an angel ministering to human needs was the appearance of one of those holy messengers to an Egyptian woman. She had become pregnant, but through no fault of her own. Both Abraham and Sarah agreed that Hagar should serve as a concubine. But even though Sarah was a party to the pregnancy, she was unwilling to accept it. Life in Abraham's home became unbearable, so Hagar fled to the wilderness.

Now that is a tough situation for any woman to be in—no home, no husband, no father to claim her unborn child, no food or medical care. Her situation was hopeless, humanly speaking. But just then something wonderful happened—"The angel of the LORD found her" (Genesis 16: 1-13). Yes, and about fifteen years later that experience repeated itself (Genesis 21:14-20). That is the way the inspired record tells it, and I believe it. And I know that Hagar thanked God for His good angels.

We all are familiar with the Biblical story of Daniel in the lions' den. Daniel was a brave and courageous man who had lived a good and godly life. By means of a clever ruse of his enemies, Daniel was accused of breaking a law of the Medes and Persians, and he was cast into a den of hungry lions, where he spent an entire night. Very early the next morning King Darius hurried to the den expecting to find a dead and devoured Daniel. But to his surprise, Daniel was alive and the lions were as meek as lambs with a case of lockjaw. Now there was a baffling miracle if ever there was one. But allow Daniel to tell what happened: "My God hath sent His angel, and hath shut the lions' mouths, that they have not hurt me: forasmuch as before Him innocency was found in me; and also before thee, O king, have I done no hurt" (Daniel 6:16-22). Knowing Daniel, according to the inspired record, I am sure he thanked God for good angels.

A few years ago, at the height of the Vietnam war, I was traveling in that country on a preaching mission with my friend, Robert Shelton. There was a keen sense of danger in our hearts one night in Saigon. We were guests in the receiving home of the Christian and Missionary Alliance. During that entire night the enemy fired rockets into the capital city. We were both exhausted and in need of sleep, but sleep that night was unthinkable. The rockets were striking so close to our house that we decided to get into a closet for safety. There was scarcely enough room for the two of us to sit in a crouched position, but there we sat. Bob kept his cassette recorder going so as to pick up the sounds of the explosions.

Added to the horrors of war was my sense of fear and loneliness. I thought of my family ten thousand miles away, wondering if I would see them again this side of Heaven. Suddenly there flashed into my mind the first "fear not" in the Bible. God had said to Abram, "Fear not, Abram: I am thy shield" (Genesis 15:1). At that very second I was aware of the presence of a third Person in that small closet. I turned to my friend and said, "Bob, all is well. We are not alone."

The following morning at breakfast Bob made reference to the fact that I slept so soundly, sitting in a crouched position in that hot closet. I believed then, and I still believe, that an angel of God put in his presence that night. I thank God for His good angels.

ANGELS MINISTERED IN CHRIST'S BEHALF

The ministry of angels is closely related to the life of our Lord Jesus Christ. An angel appeared to Joseph assuring him that Mary was still a virgin and that her pregnancy was the result of the Holy Spirit's supernatural intervention (Matthew 1:18-25). Angels appeared to the shepherds as they watched over their flocks, announcing the birth of Jesus (Luke 2:8-20). As always, their message was in detail and accurate, for we are told that "the shepherds returned, glorifying and praising God for all the things that they had heard and seen, as it was told unto them" (Luke 2:20).

I have the feeling that Joseph was pleased with his first meeting with God's good angels. But if he had any questions as to their validity and authority, those questions were answered when God's heavenly messengers came to him again. When Herod was preparing to have the small children in Bethlehem killed, an angel appeared to Joseph again, "saying, Arise, and take the young child and His mother, and flee into Egypt, and be thou there until I bring thee word: for Herod will seek the young child to destroy Him" (Matthew 2:13). Herod's rage and hatred were against the only Holy Child, the Son of God, therefore God used His special messenger to save the life of the child Jesus. Herod himself was smitten with death, and again God sent one of His heavenly creatures to give to Joseph the all-clear signal (Matthew 2:19-23). This was Joseph's third experience with God's good angels.

We do not read far into Matthew's record until we witness angels ministering directly to the Lord Jesus as a man. It happened in the wilderness when Jesus was tempted by Satan. The devil made three assaults upon Jesus, but each assault was turned back with our Lord's mighty defense, "It is written." Then Jesus said to Satan, "Get thee hence," and "the devil leaveth Him." Immediately "angels came and ministered unto Him" (Matthew 4:1-11). In exactly what way the angels ministered to our Lord we are not told. We do know that He faced Satan, hunger, and "wild beasts" (Mark 1:13), so that we have reason to believe that those good angels ministered to His physical needs.

Jesus was "strengthened" by an angel during His agony and suffering in the garden of Gethsemane (Luke 22:43). After Christ's resurrection an angel of the Lord came to remove the stone from the entrance to His tomb to show that He was risen and the tomb was empty, and to give an assuring word to the women (Matthew 28:1-8; see also John 20:11-14). Yes, the risen Lord was "seen of angels" (1 Timothy 3:16) in His birth, boyhood, baptism, battles, His bodily resurrection, and His ascension to Heaven where He is now "so much better than the angels" (Hebrews 1:4).

Angels are close observers of all activity on the earth. They rejoice every time a sinner receives the Lord Jesus Christ as Saviour. Jesus said, "Likewise, I say unto you, there is joy in the presence of the angels of God over one sinner that repenteth" (Luke 15:10).

Angels have an active part in the departure of believers from this life at the death of the body. "And it came to pass, that the beggar died, and was carried by the angels into Abraham's bosom" (Luke 16:22).

Angels will serve Christ in the judgment of unbelievers at the end of the age. Jesus said, "The field is the world; the good seed are the children of the kingdom; but the tares are the children of the wicked one; The enemy that sowed them is the devil; the harvest is the end of the world; and the reapers are the angels" (Matthew 13:38-39; see also Luke 12:8-9).

Angels will accompany Christ when He returns to earth in His glory. "For the Son of man shall come in the glory of His Father with His angels; and then He shall reward every man according to his works" (Matthew 16:27).

In these days of increased demon activity, God's people need to be acquainted with His good angels and their many ministries. For the most part they are associated with the unseen world, but God has told us sufficient about them to cause us to look up and praise Him for His good angels.

THE HEART OF THE PROBLEM
AND ITS SOLUTION

The Christian Church today faces a strange crisis, something quite different from the problems that plagued her in past centuries. In the late 1800's theologians of repute tried to eliminate the supernatural from the Bible. Scriptural miracles were explained away, or else dealt with in doubtful fashion. German rationalism gave to the world the theory that the Bible contained a collection of documents, some eloquent and interesting, but that those documents were merely the impressions of the men who recorded them. It was an attack of human reason against divine revelation. That neotheology invaded the western world and produced a "new morality." Both the theology and the morality were corrupt. People who do not believe right cannot be expected to behave right.

But today we have among us men of professed evangelical spirit who are creating a serious and damaging effect upon Christ's Church. The late Joseph Parker had a way of dealing with miracles so as to leave his readers wondering if he really believed in the supernatural. I feel the same about the late Dean Stanley. However, today we have men who play up the supernatural and the miraculous. They draw large crowds with demonstrations of "miracles" and success stories. Paperback books telling of God's exploits appear almost daily, replacing the gospel of the grace of God in salvation with the gospel of success and the gospel of experience.

Herein lies the problem in the current crisis. The new satanic counterfeit cuts across denominational and synodical lines. The recent religious revolution is a total one, involving Jews, Roman Catholics, and Protestants. The monster of barbaric communism is an evil, as deadly and devastating as ever, but presently it is sitting by, laughing at the devil's big religious bonanzas. I must confess that inwardly I have no feeling of elation over the reports of big crowds, large collections of money, and bodily healings. And believe me, my feelings cannot be charged to "sour grapes" on my part.

I have too many questions about the religious life of our present generation, especially in a world so conscious of witchcraft, tarot cards, the crystal ball, astrology, the ouija board, and other forms of Satanism. Psychiatrists, psychologists, and even scientists are studying reports of supernatural phenomena. Colleges and universities are adding new courses in occultism. This is an age of phenomenal progress in the occult in highly civilized countries, an evil practice that until recently was confined to backward, undeveloped tribes people.

The history of true Christianity is a record of deliverance from the bonds of Satan and demons. When a sinner was saved in the early days of the Church, he was unshackled from demonism, from "the prince of the power of the air, the spirit that now worketh in the children of disobedience" (Ephesians 2:2). The regenerated man was "delivered . . . from the power of darkness" (Colossians 1:13). In Ephesus the converts to Jesus Christ, "which used curious arts brought their books together, and burned them before all men: and they counted the price of them, and found it fifty thousand pieces of silver" (Acts 19:19). The public burning of those magical scrolls was one way of testifying openly that the persons involved were delivered from Satanism to Christ.

Those who became Christians consented together to declare themselves free of any loyalty to Satan.

Occultism was rife in Ephesus in Paul's day. But the preaching of the Word of God in the power of the Holy Spirit overcame the powers of evil. There were the exorcists who made merchandise of casting out evil spirits (19:13). But evidence seems to indicate a clear cleavage between the Holy Spirit and evil spirits. And look at the final results: "So mightily grew the Word of God and prevailed" (Acts 19:20).

The special miracles which God wrought through Paul were by no means an encouragement to become involved in the Satan-worship of that time. On the other hand, Paul's ministry encouraged and expanded the study of God's Word. The pure Word of God is the only answer to the practitioners of magic and witchcraft. The powers of darkness were dispelled by the invasion of the truth. The genuine fruit of the pure Word of God is the turning of men from their sins and satanic devices, and the beginning of a new life.

The magicmongers are with us today. But it is a sad commentary on the state of the Church when God's children are labeled by professing Christians as being unloving and ungracious because they will not condone the charismatic cult of Satan's domain. We need to learn from the Apostle Paul. The Satan-cult of Paul's day performed in "the name of the Lord Jesus" (Acts 19:13), but the apostle of Christ was neither deceived by Satan's ministers, nor did he soft-pedal the gospel. As a result of Paul's firm stand, the Word of God spread with force and rapidity. Had Paul compromised, we would not have Luke's message of the mighty conquest of truth. It is not un-Christlike to insist that divine truth take precedence over fleshly or satanic experiences.

This brings me to my main burden. What has caused the strange phenomenon we are witnessing in Christendom today? I believe the great fault of our times is neglect of the Bible. We have more paraphrases, translations, amplifications, versions, and perversions of the Bible than the world has ever seen. We have more conventions, retreats, clinics, conferences, and rallies than ever before. The competition to become the largest, the fastest growing, and most widely known has never been so keen. But when it is all put together, there remains a tragic dearth of Bible knowledge. Our churches hire educated specialists for every department of the church and Sunday school, but when it comes to knowing and understanding the Word of God, we have never had so much educated ignorance. The great need of the Church today is a revival of a consistent, consecutive, systematic, personal study of the Bible

The late D. L. Moody was mightily used of God, yet he once said, "If I had my life to live over, I would pray less and study my Bible more." No Christian ever prayed his way through a book in the Bible. As necessary as prayer is to spiritual growth, a diligent study of the Scriptures is indispensable. The Christian who does not study the Bible is lacking in spiritual discernment. There is something seriously wrong with the professing Christian who has no desire to read and study and understand God's Word. The Word of God constitutes the food of the new nature. The Apostle Peter wrote, "As newborn babes, desire the sincere milk of the Word, that ye may grow thereby" (1 Peter 2:2).

The Christian who fails to give attention to his spiritual diet is lacking in nutrition and growth. Simple Bible study has given way to creeds, confessions, catechisms, cults, and controversies. Failing to feed on the Scriptures we fail to understand them, and this failure results in becoming entangled with Satan's counterfeit. Literally millions of modern paraphrases and translations have been purchased in the past twenty years. Many purchasers had the idea that some new translation would prove to be a short-cut to understanding the Bible. In May 1967 *Reader's Digest* published an article entitled, "At Last: One Bible For All Christians." Many persons bought that Bible, but the mere fact that they own a copy of it will do them no good.

The exhortation to "desire [long for] the sincere milk of the Word" is not to be treated lightly. The adjective "sincere" (Greek, *adolos*) means pure and unadulterated, guileless. The word "guileless" here is in direct contrast to "all guile," which we are told to put away (2:1). The words in the Bible which make up *the* Word of God are pure words (Psalm 12:6; 19:8; 119:140), meaning they are undefiled, uncontaminated. It is the unadulterated food of God's Word that ministers to growth, and guards the mind from heresy. It matters not what men say about the Bible, but rather what the Bible says. Know what the Bible says and what it means and you will never get caught in Satan's sieve. The strongest bulwark against bad doctrine and bad deportment is to know the Scriptures. Ignorance of the Scriptures is the cause of all evil. The Word of God will purge out the evil that is in the mind as well as prevent other evils from entering the mind.

"Husbands, love your wives, even as Christ also loved the church, and gave Himself for it; That He might sanctify and cleanse it with the washing of water by the Word" (Ephesians 5:25-26). "Wherewithal shall a young man cleanse his way? by taking heed thereto according to Thy Word" (Psalm 119:9). "Thy Word have I hid in mine heart, that I might not sin against Thee" (Psalm 119:11).

We get closer to the heart of the problem in Paul's word to Timothy: "Study to shew thyself approved unto God, a workman that needeth not to be ashamed, rightly dividing the Word of truth" (2 Timothy 2:15).

Paul suggests that there are two kinds of workmen in this business of religion. On the one hand, there are those who stand before God "approved . . . not ashamed." On the other hand, there are those who are disapproved and ought to be deeply ashamed of themselves. The difference between the two is in their handling of "the Word of truth."

The good workman with God's approval is the one who is "rightly dividing the Word of truth." "Rightly dividing" is the translation of the Greek verb, *orthotomeō,* meaning to handle rightly so as to cut straight. The word occurs this once only in the New Testament. What is intended in this one reference is rightly dealing with Scripture, teaching Scripture accurately. Arndt and Gingrich render it, "to cut a path in a straight direction." Today people are going in many different directions along the religious freeways, because there are too many men and women peddling their religious wares who do not know the Word of truth. They falsify the truth, thereby confusing the people.

Paul met one of those false teachers, "Elymas the sorcerer" (Acts 13:8). Elymas was a wizard who pretended to have powers of magic, but he did not know God's Word. He was a perverter of the truth, who made crooked the straight paths of the Lord. A renegade Jew, whose correct name was Bar-Jesus, he was involved in all sorts of magic and quackery. Mincing no words, Paul said to him, "O full of all subtilty and all mischief, thou child of the devil, thou enemy of all righteousness, wilt thou not cease to pervert the right ways of the Lord?" (Acts 13:10)

This man was a charlatan, a child of the devil, an enemy of all that is right and good. By misrepresenting and misapplying the truth, he perverted the truth. We see all around us today those who, like Elymas the sorcerer, have so yielded themselves to satanic influence that they lead others away from God's truth.

In view of the growing list of false teachers and teachers who teach false doctrines, there is need for real teachers of the truth. Men are needed who have studied, been tested, and been made fit for service by God. The man who rightly divides God's Word ploughs a straight road through the truth. The perverters of the truth claim progress, but their progress is in reverse. They preach and claim miracles, but they leave their followers befogged when it comes to understanding the Bible. The most effective refutation of error is truth. Oh, how we need to discipline ourselves in the study of God's Word so that we might unblushingly submit our ministry to God for His approval! We must be scrupulously honest in dealing with God's Word.

Here is a classic example of perverting the truth. In March 1974 I was in Detroit to minister in the Highland Park Baptist Church. From 1956 to 1963 I had served as pastor of that church. While there during this most recent visit, a man asked me if I had ever spoken in tongues. When I replied that I had not, he responded with a quick, "Why not?" I told him that for forty-seven years God and I had gotten along quite well in English. We communicated with each other by means of prayer and the Bible, and the relationship had proved very successful.

This comment seemed to upset him somewhat. When he recovered sufficiently to manage a comeback, he said, "Speaking in tongues is a valid New Testament experience, and since you haven't spoken in tongues you do not have all that God wants you to have. How can you teach others when you are short on experience?"

I could tell from the twinkle in his eye he thought he had me. But it was now my turn to do the questioning.

"Is raising the dead a valid New Testament experience?" I asked. He agreed that it was.

"Have you ever raised anyone from the dead?" He admitted he had not.

But I was not about to let go. I pressed him with the

next question, "Is walking on the water a valid New Testament experience?" He agreed that it was.

"Have you ever walked on the water?" He said that he had not.

Desirous of helping him, I softened my approach. I then asked him, "Would you say that because you have not raised anyone from the dead nor walked on water you do not have all that God wants you to have?" He was speechless.

His problem reflects a serious illness in the churches, namely an ignorance of, and the inability rightly to divide, the Word of truth. It is not possible for one to get the truth if one cannot rightly divide it. Serious questions must be asked concerning any statement in a text, such as, Who said it? To whom was it said? For example, it was Jesus who told a man to walk on the water. But whom did He tell to do it? Peter, of course. How ridiculous it would be for any of us to try such a feat! Jesus did not tell you or me to walk on the water. For those who preach that all such miracles must be duplicated today, it might be a good thing for us all if they went offshore about fifty miles and tried walking on the water (not with a millstone about his neck. See Matthew 18:6).

The Bible does not yield up its treasures to the casual, careless reader. Understanding the Bible does not require a course in philosophy, psychology, art, science, or any of the other branches of learning. It is its own interpreter, asking only that we heed its "words . . . which the Holy Ghost teacheth; comparing spiritual things with spiritual" (1 Corinthians 2:13). Modern education, without the Bible, fails utterly in its attempt to teach us about our world, life, and human nature. Given a chance, the Bible will reveal its own message in its own way. Spiritual truth is made known by the Holy Spirit (1 Corinthians 2:10) to spiritual men (1 Corinthians 2:14). Some natural (unregenerated) men are having a lot to say about the Bible, but they must be written off as untrustworthy. The devil quoted Scripture in support of his attack against the Lord Jesus Christ (Matthew 4:6), but he was using the Word of God to try to influence our Lord to do a right thing with a wrong motive.

The essential *need* in man, before he can understand and interpret the Scriptures, is that he be born again. The change is a radical one, I agree; however our Lord insisted upon it (John 3:3-7). Without this experience of regeneration it is impossible to grasp the truth of divine revelation. "But the natural man receiveth not the things of the Spirit of God: for they are foolishness unto him: neither can he know them, because they are spiritually discerned" (1 Corinthians 2:14).

The natural (Greek, *psuchikos*) man knows only those values that are physical and material. He is ignorant of what lies beyond the physical and material, therefore he evaluates everything from physical and material standards. Paul says that a man like that cannot understand spiritual things. A man as he is by nature (a natural man) is dominated purely by natural reasoning. No matter how intellectual or intelligent, he really has no capacity to discern spiritual truth. How dark is that mind which is still under Satan's control! To him the precepts, parables, and prophecies in the Bible are foolishness.

Right here one finds the answer to the question, Why is there so much confusion in the religious world? "The god of this world [world system] hath blinded the minds of them which believe not" (2 Corinthians 4:4). "Having the understanding darkened, being alienated from the life of God through the ignorance that is in them, because of the blindness of their heart" (Ephesians 4:18).

A scholar can be a genius in natural knowledge, and yet be totally ignorant of the Word of God. God's truth he *"cannot know,"* a fact that is objectively true about him. He needs to be converted, saved, born again.

The essential *source* of information and interpretation of the Bible is the Holy Spirit. He is the Author of the written Word of God. "All scripture is given by inspiration of God, and is profitable for doctrine, for reproof, for correction, for instruction in righteousness" (2 Timothy 3:16).

The word "inspiration" appears here only in the New Testament. It is the translation of *theopneustos*, meaning "God-breathed, or God-inspired." There are many *man-made* writings expounding and supporting Satan's heresies, but those only tend to draw man away from God. The one Book to help man get free from Satan and bring him to God is the Bible. Every man needs to be converted, convicted of error, and corrected, and the Scriptures when rightly understood will get the job done. It is this special "inspiration" which is the secret of the Bible's power. The Bible has the stamp of divine truth and power upon it throughout, and that is the first thing every man must know and accept.

The essential *teacher* of the Scriptures is the Holy Spirit. One of the last promises of our Saviour before His crucifixion was the teaching ministry of the Holy Spirit. In the upper room Jesus said, "I have yet many things to say unto you, but ye cannot bear them now. Howbeit when He, the Spirit of truth, is come, He will guide you into all truth: for He shall not speak of Himself; but whatsoever He shall hear, that shall He speak: and He will shew you things to come. He shall glorify Me: for He shall receive of Mine, and shall shew it unto you. All things that the Father hath are Mine: therefore said I, that He shall take of Mine, and shall shew it unto you" (John 16:12-15).

When our Lord spoke these words this particular ministry of the Holy Spirit was yet future. It had its beginning on the Day of Pentecost and continues throughout the church age. The content of His teaching ministry embraces "all *the* truth" (the definite article is in the Greek text), including the Person of Christ, the precepts for daily life, and prophecy ("things to come"). We can depend upon the Divine Teacher to reveal what is necessary for us to know because Jesus said, "He shall teach you all things" (John 14:26). "But as it is written, Eye hath not seen, nor ear heard, neither have entered into the heart of man, the things which God hath prepared for them that love Him. But God hath revealed them unto us by His Spirit: for the Spirit searcheth all things, yea, the deep things of God" (1 Corinthians 2:9-10).

There are things perceived by the senses, the eye, the ear, and the mind, but such things do not include divinely revealed truth. The secrets of God are revealed "unto us," namely "them that love Him," and the Revealer is the Holy Spirit who only is capable of making known the mysteries of God's wisdom. Both the inspiration and revelation of the Scriptures are accomplished by the Holy Spirit. This ought to be enough to warn every man of the impossibility of any of us understanding divine truth independent of the Divine Teacher. The Christian is exhorted to "study, search, read, and meditate," but all our efforts in pursuing the truth must be in the spirit of dependence upon the Holy Spirit.

The essential *attitude* of the learner of Scripture is important. If we are to gain a knowledge of God's Word we must come to the Bible with a broken spirit and confess every known sin. I am afraid that many of us are careless about this important matter of personal holiness. The Apostle James gives to his readers a worthful suggestion when he says, "Wherefore lay apart all filthiness and superfluity of naughtiness, and receive with meekness the engrafted Word, which is able to save your souls" (James 1:21).

Every form of uncleanness, whether in thought, word, or deed must be pulled out by the roots. That rank growth of weeds must be removed if the good seed of God's Word is to produce fruit in our lives. The foul, rank growth of malice, jealousy, prejudice, selfishness, and carnality must be cleared away. The Word of God is holy seed, and it must have clean soil.

The Word must be received with meekness, with a docile and open mind, not with the attitude of a know-it-all. There can be no intrusion of self if the Word is to become fruitful. There is no point in reading and studying the Bible if I am determined to live my life in my own way. Every truly converted person brings with him into his new life his old unregenerated nature, his depraved self. This must give way to the new Commander in Chief, the Holy Spirit. God's Word is a living message to man's heart, but we must receive it "as it is in truth, the Word of God, which effectually worketh also in you that believe" (1 Thessalonians 2:13). Yes, the Bible works in the meek and believing heart.

The devil knows how to get us sidetracked. He might confuse the issue as he did with Eve (Genesis 3:1-5); or he might steal the seed of God's Word before it takes root in the heart (Mark 4:14-15); or he might quote Scripture, as in his assault upon our Lord (Matthew 4:6); or he might sow "tares" (his children) among the "good seed" (the children of God's kingdom) (Matthew 13:24-30; 36-43). Yes, he is an expert in knowing what to do with God's Word.

THE ESSENTIAL INGREDIENT

"But be ye doers of the Word, and not hearers only, deceiving your own selves" (James 1:22). Reading, hearing sermons, and even studying God's Word are not an end in themselves. When the Word heard and studied is never obeyed, this becomes a form of self-deception. We need to become good students of Bible truth but we cannot be "hearers only." We must be "doers" as well. Our Lord pronounced a blessing upon them "that hear the Word of God, and keep it" (Luke 11:28). The difference between hearing and doing God's Word is emphasized in our Lord's parable of the sower, the seed, and the soils. He said, "Take heed *what* ye hear: with what measure ye mete, it shall be measured to you: and unto you that hear shall more be given" (Mark 4:24). "Take heed therefore *how* ye hear: for whosoever hath, to him shall be given; and whosoever hath not, from him shall be taken even that which he seemeth to have" (Luke 8:18). "My mother and My brethren are these which hear the Word of God, and do it" (Luke 8:21).

If we content ourselves with the preacher's ability or personality, or with the enjoyment of an emotional kick, or with the excitement of watching a miracle performed, or with the novelty of listening to someone babble incomprehensibly, we are indeed in serious trouble and a victim of Satan's devices.

The true student is one who considers seriously the implication and application of God's Word for practical Christian living. Our Lord said, "If any man will do . . . he shall know (John 7:17). Disobedience is a major hindrance to understanding God's Word. There are people who claim they believe the Bible, yet they neither understand it nor obey it. Faith in the Word of God means a knowledge of that Word and obedience to it.

God's Word is not an end in itself. God's commands must be followed by our obedience. There are two alternative responses to the Word of God: they are the pathway of obedience and the pathway of disobedience. Observing the commands of Scripture is an indispensable condition of true discipleship. Jesus concluded His Sermon on the Mount with the following words: "Therefore whosoever heareth these sayings of Mine, and doeth them, I will liken him unto a wise man, which built his house upon a rock: And the rain descended, and the floods came, and the winds blew, and beat upon that house; and it fell not; for it was founded upon a rock. And everyone that heareth these sayings of Mine, and doeth them not, shall be likened unto a foolish man, which built his house upon the sand: And the rain descended, and the floods came, and winds blew, and beat upon that house; and it fell: and great was the fall of it" (Matthew 7:24-27).

Here we have a practical discourse on the difference between "hearing" and "doing." There are but two roads to choose between, not many. There is grave peril in refusing to obey, a lesson Adam and Eve learned too late. There are crowning rewards for all who obey God's Word. It is through the Scriptures, and through these alone, that men discover God's will and the blessings which attend all who follow His will. It is through ignorance of the Scriptures that people become involved in Satan's program. The person who chooses to take from the Bible what pleases him and neglects what is distasteful to him is already Satan's dupe. As the blueprint and specifications guide the builder in the erection of the building, so the Word of God will guide the earnest seeker after truth. You can't afford to neglect the Bible.

COMPLETE IN CHRIST

The Epistle to the Colossians, strange as it might seem, was written to bring to a halt a great religious revival. Like all religious revivals, this one had Satan as its leader. Let me remind you that I make the clear distinction between religion and Christianity. Christ is the founder and head of Christianity. Satan is the founder and head of all religion. There is a marked difference between these two systems.

Christianity is truth because Christ is the Truth (John 14:6), and the truth always makes men free (John 8:32). All religion is false because its founder is the father of lies (John 8:44); thus religion blinds men to the truth, thereby holding them in spiritual bondage. So whenever Satan wants to launch an all-out attack against Christ and the truth, he starts a religious revival. You see, religion is the devil's counterfeit for the truth.

Now I am not so much as suggesting that the religions of the world have no truth in them. To the contrary, I must agree that they all have a mixture of some truth with their system of error, else they could not gain so many followers.

The devil is a very religious person. The fall of Lucifer, whereby he became the devil, was the result of his attempt to dethrone God and enthrone himself. He said, "I will ascend into heaven, I will exalt my throne above the stars of God: I will sit also upon the mount of the congregation, in the sides of the north: I will ascend above the heights of the clouds;

I will be like the most High" (Isaiah 14:13-14).

Why did the angel Lucifer want to be like God? He wanted to be worshiped. This is brought out clearly in the testing of Christ in the wilderness, for we read, "Again, the devil taketh Him up into an exceeding high mountain, and sheweth Him all the kingdoms of the world, and the glory of them; And saith unto Him, All these things will I give Thee, if Thou wilt fall down and worship me" (Matthew 4:8-9).

This worship of men's hearts, which Satan seeks, will reach its zenith in the tribulation after the true Church has been caught up from the earth to Heaven. At that time all on the whole inhabited earth, whose names are not written in the Lamb's book of life, will worship the devil. A refusal on the part of anyone will result in death (Revelation 13:4, 8,15).

In the meantime, Satan keeps active in the realm of religion. His program never lags. He, whom our Lord called "the prince of this world" (John 14:30; 16:11), and whom Paul designated, "the god of this world," is relentlessly busy in religious revivals by which he has "blinded the minds of them which believe not, lest the light of the glorious gospel of Christ, who is the image of God, should shine unto them" (2 Corinthians 4:4). The world of religion is overrun with "false apostles, deceitful workers, transforming themselves into the apostles of Christ. And no marvel; for Satan himself is transformed into an angel of light. Therefore it is no great thing if his ministers also be transformed as the ministers of righteousness; whose end shall be according to their works" (2 Corinthians 11:13-15).

Satan's method of blinding men to the truth is by means of a *syncretism.* The dictionary defines a *syncretism* as a union of conflicting religious beliefs. It is a movement to unite different religions by seeking some common ground for coalescence.

In the city of Colosse, in Asia Minor, Satan instigated and inspired a philosophy called Gnosticism. It was a syncretism made up of Judaistic legalism, Roman paganism, Hellenistic philosophy, and the vocabulary of Christianity. Not Christianity, but merely the *vocabulary* of Christianity. By injecting a little of the right vocabulary, Satan's victims fell an easy prey to his new religion. The intellectual pride of the Gnostics had watered down the pure gospel of redemption through Christ into a philosophy. This group, by flaunting its new intellectualism and "science falsely so called" (1 Timothy 6:20), led the less educated ones to believe that their neognosticism possessed a superior knowledge.

Thus Paul wrote by inspiration, "And this I say, lest any man should beguile you with enticing words" (Colossians 2:4). "Beware lest any man spoil you through philosophy and vain deceit, after the tradition of men, after the rudiments of the world, and not after Christ" (Colossians 2:8). Paul was warning the church at Colosse, and us, to beware of any merger of world religions which appeals with "enticing words," that is, words which sound good and which might lead one to believe that this new syncretism will solve all of life's problems.

Now who might turn from the religion he is practicing to a new syncretism? Only that person whose religion is not meeting all of his needs, the incomplete person who is restless and dissatisfied. Perhaps most of the people in this present generation, if they are honest, will admit that their lives are incomplete. Never in the history of the human race have there been so many frustrated people. With the turn of the century there was a fantastic growth and development of psychology, the science which treats of the traits, feelings, and actions of the mind. Men and women are spending millions of dollars annually in fees paid to psychologists, psychiatrists, and professional counselors as they seek release from their frustrations.

The emotional ills of the masses provide Satan with an opportunity to introduce a new cult, or a religious syncretism. We are witnessing the phenomenal rise of the cults of tongues and healing. Never in the history of the Christian Church has there been such a widespread interest in religious mergers. The devil's one-world church is coming into international prominence and acceptance. Who are the people who are running to tongues and healing meetings? Who are the people who blindly ally themselves with Satan's syncretism? Only the fearful, incomplete, dissatisfied persons whose religion is not meeting their needs. These are following the modern approach of psychology: If you are dissatisfied with your present location, move elsewhere. If you are restless in your job, quit and look for another. If you are frustrated in your marriage, get a divorce and begin again with someone else. But psychology has not succeeded in explaining man's behavior, nor does it have the solution to man's frustrations.

For example, in 1963 an incomplete, unhappy, frustrated woman divorced her husband, a respected and successful medical doctor, and walked out on her four children, that she might be free to seek completeness through living with another man. She married a famous and wealthy man, not, of course, until after he divorced his wife. In the first year of her new marriage, this incomplete woman still was not happy. Being free from her first husband and children, and having been rocketed to fame, this frustrated woman sought custody of her four children. She found a substitute for that which she had, only to discover that the substitute added no permanent happiness. Modern psychology proved inadequate to provide completeness.

All of us need the completeness that is found only in Jesus Christ, "For in Him dwelleth all the *fulness* of the

Godhead bodily. And ye are complete in Him, which is the head of all principality and power" (Colossians 2:9-10). This word "fullness" (Greek, *pleroma*) means perfect, complete, wanting nothing. The believing sinner, who trusts implicitly in Christ, discovers that he is fully satisfied and wants nothing, and this is precisely what is meant by the words, "ye are *complete* in Him." The marginal reading correctly translates "complete" to read, "filled up." Jesus Christ is the only complete man who ever lived, and apart from Him we are incomplete. But the moment we trust in Him, something happens inside us that provides the real meaning of life.

The very heart of the Colossian letter is its doctrine of the *pleroma* or "fullness." It is a divine attribute, so that God is its Author and Source. One of the purposes of the Incarnation was to make the divine completeness available for our human incompleteness. Christ came in order that He might fill us with the fullness of God.

But first, we must see this fullness in Christ Himself. The Holy Spirit says, "For it pleased the Father that in Him should all *fulness* dwell" (Colossians 1:19). And then He adds, "For in Him dwelleth all the *fulness* of the Godhead bodily" (Colossians 2:9). Do not miss this tremendous truth, namely that nothing can be added to the God-Man, our Lord and Saviour Jesus Christ. He is complete in Himself. That is eternally true, for Christ was, is, and ever will be fully God. He is "the same yesterday, and to day, and for ever" (Hebrews 13:8). He possesses all the necessary qualifications to be man's complete and perfect Saviour. All that God is, Jesus Christ is. "And without controversy great is the mystery of godliness: God was manifest in the flesh" (1 Timothy 3:16).

All the unbounded powers and provisions of deity are in Jesus Christ. He is the one sole temple of the fullness of

God. He lacks nothing. And since that is true, why should we go anywhere else or look to anyone else? God purposed that through Christ His fullness should be passed on to you and me. The obvious intentional plan of the Father in sending His Son to earth is that man, being incomplete because of sin, might be made complete in Christ. All the fullness of God is in Him, that from Him it may come to us. This treasure of completeness was placed in the earthen vessel of our Lord's manhood that it might be within reach of every man.

Don't miss it! The only reason some of you have missed it until now is because you have not received Christ. Think not for one single moment that a change of environment, or location, or marital status, or meeting new people, or seeing new faces can make you complete. Though all the earth were one beautiful and peaceful spring day every day, and all the people on earth cared for you and loved you, and the wealth of the earth were at your disposal, you would still be incomplete. You need more than creature help; you need more than financial help. You need the fullness of God from which you can draw day by day. And that fullness is all in Christ for each of us.

"That ye might be filled with all the fulness of God" (Ephesians 3:19) was the burden of Epaphras, whom Paul described as "a servant of Christ . . . always labouring fervently for you in prayers, that ye may stand perfect and complete [filled up] in all the will of God" (Colossians 4:12). That stream of divine fullness, like the eternal river of life, flows from the heart of the living Saviour, and it is available to you and me.

Don't turn to any cult or religion when all the fullness is in the blessed Son of God. Don't run from your marital difficulty to a divorce court when you and your mate in marriage can be made complete in Christ. Don't contemplate suicide when the Saviour can give you abundant life.

Are you weary and tired of your present way of life? Jesus said, "Come unto Me, all ye that labour and are heavy laden, and I will give you rest" (Matthew 11:28).

Are you at a loss to know which way to turn? The Bible says, "In whom [Christ] are hid all the treasures of wisdom and knowledge" (Colossians 2:3).

Are you sick of your life of sin? In Him "we have redemption through His blood, even the forgiveness of sins" (Colossians 1:14).

Trust Christ and draw from His fullness. He can make you complete.

Two mighty truths, intended for the Colossians (and for us), are: all the fullness (or completeness) of the Godhead is in Christ; all the fullness (or completeness) of Christ is available to us. These two fabulous facts lay at the very heart of the Colossian Epistle. And what a message they contain! "In Him dwelleth all the *fulness* of the Godhead bodily; and ye are *filled—full* in Him."

Here is the one and only final reply to the hawkers of cults, psychology, philosophies, science falsely so-called, and religious mergers which refuse to accept the divine declaration that Christ is fully God, and therefore fully capable of undertaking all the affairs of those who trust Him.